The
Reading/Writing
Teacher's
Companion

EXPLORE
POETRY

The Reading/Writing Teacher's Companion

Investigate Nonfiction
Experiment with Fiction
Discover Your Own Literacy
Build a Literate Classroom
Explore Poetry

The
Reading/Writing
Teacher's
Companion

EXPLORE
POETRY

Donald H. Graves

HEINEMANN
Portsmouth, NH

IRWIN PUBLISHING
Toronto, Canada

Heinemann Educational Books, Inc.
361 Hanover Street   Portsmouth, NH 03801-3959
Offices and agents throughout the world

Published simultaneously in Canada by
Irwin Publishing
1800 Steeles Avenue West   Concord, Ontario, Canada L4K 2P3

Acknowledgments for borrowed material begin on p. xiv.

Every effort has been made to contact the copyright holders for permission to reprint borrowed material. We regret any oversights that may have occurred and would be happy to rectify them in future printings of this work.

Library of Congress Cataloging-in-Publication Data

Graves, Donald H.
    Explore poetry / Donald H. Graves.
        p.   cm.—(The Reading/writing teacher's companion)
    Includes bibliographical references and index.
    ISBN 0-435-08489-5
    1. Poetry—Study and teaching (Elementary)—United States. 2. Poetry—Authorship—Study and teaching (Elementary)—United States.
    I. Title. II. Series: Graves, Donald H. Reading/writing teacher's companion.
    LB1576.G7275   1992
    372.6'4—dc20   92-3333
                                                CIP

Canadian Cataloguing in Publication Data

Graves, Donald H.
    Explore poetry

(The Reading/writing teacher's companion)
Includes bibliographical references and index.
ISBN 0-7725-1933-1

1. Poetry—Study and teaching. I. Title.
II. Series: Graves, Donald H. The reading/writing teacher's companion.

PN1101.G73   1992   808.1'07   C92-093672-5

Designed by Wladislaw Finne.
Back-cover photo by Mekeel McBride.
Printed in the United States of America.
10 9 8 7 6 5 4 3 2 1

To
Betty Lewis Graves

---

*Who sees the world as a garden
filled with poems*

contents

8   Choral Speaking and the Learning of Poems 143

9   Poetry Belongs Throughout the Curriculum 153

about this series

Reading and writing are both composing processes. History shows they have been kept apart. This series, The Reading/Writing Teacher's Companion, brings them together. With these books as a guide, you can explore the richness of reading and writing for yourself and for children. You can improve your own listening, experiment with learning, and recognize children's potential in reading and writing. Five books make up the series:

- *Investigate Nonfiction.*
- *Experiment with Fiction.*
- *Discover Your Own Literacy.*
- *Build a Literate Classroom.*
- *Explore Poetry.*

The approach to teaching and learning is basically the same in all five books, although each stands alone in its focus. All five emphasize a learning style that immediately engages you in trying literacy for yourself, then the children. So much of learning is, and ought to be, experimental. A series of "Actions," experiments for personal growth and discovery in the classroom, are highlighted in the text to help you develop the kind of literate classroom you want. The Actions are ordered in such a way that you will gradually become aware of children's growing independence in some aspect of literacy. In all five books I'll be trying the experiments right along with you.

The five books stress learning within a literate community. Reading and writing are social acts in which children and teachers together share the books and authors they enjoy and their own composing in the various genres. Make no mistake, individuals are important, but good classrooms have always stressed group as well as individual responsibility.

The books also stress the importance of your own learning within a community. When you try the Actions and enter into new experiments with your teaching, you ought to consider reading and learning with colleagues in order to maximize your own efforts to grow as a professional.

xi

acknowl-edgments

Four years ago I went back to school to take a course in writing poetry. The course was taught by Mekeel McBride, associate professor of English at the University of New Hampshire. Mekeel is a distinguished poet with her work found in leading poetry journals. She published three books with Carnegie Mellon in the 1980s. I was struck by her knowledge of poetry and what I was able to do as a fledgling writer in the genre. I was struck even more by her approach to the teaching of poetry.

Her approach was simple and persuasive: write poetry rapidly and daily; share regularly; and surround yourself with poetry of all kinds. She quickly built a community of writers who learned to help each other. She conferred with each of us individually and seemed to see more in our writing than we could see ourselves. She kept us in touch with our voices and our potential. There was always a reason to go back to work. I am grateful to her and my colleagues in the course. I experienced firsthand the effect of her teaching both in the class and in our discussions over the next three years.

My wife, Betty, to whom this book is dedicated, has responded in her usual no-nonsense, but encouraging, way to just about every poem and chapter when they were first written. It takes an unusual person to respond to first drafts.

Georgia Heard, author of *For the Good of the Earth and Sun*, has shown me a poet's stance to the world and to children. I am grateful to her for her patient responses to my attempts to be a poet as well as her own work in the field with children and schools.

Don Murray continually responded to my poetry, offering encouragement and specific suggestions to the text. Nancie Atwell and Jane Hansen were helpful respondents to various chapters and poems.

University students, particularly Lisa Noble, showed me how they learned to think and write as poets. Children in many places in the country, from Colorado to New Hampshire, were instructive with their fresh voices. Margaret Pelczar, first-grade teacher in Moultonboro, New Hampshire, showed me what first-grade children could do with poetry.

Explore Poetry is the last of five books in The Reading/Writing Teacher's Companion series. The series began as one book, grew to three, and then to five, because of my editor, Philippa Stratton. She had both the vision, the patience, and the right amount of encouragement to see all five books through to completion. This book, and the series, would not have happened without her.

I am grateful to Donna Bouvier and Joanne Tranchemontagne from Heinemann, who saw to the details and maintained the spirit a book needs to be completed.

The author and publisher wish to thank the following for permission to reprint previously published material:

Page 10: From Mark Irwin, *The Halo of Desire* (Baltimore, MD: Galileo Press, 1987). Reprinted by permission of the author.

Page 12: From Marge Piercy, *My Mother's Body*. Copyright © 1985 by Marge Piercy. Reprinted by permission of Alfred A. Knopf, Inc.

Page 13: From Robert Francis, *The Orb Weaver*. Copyright © 1960 by Robert Francis, Wesleyan University Press. Reprinted by permission of University Press of New England.

Pages 73–74: From Thomas Newkirk and Nancy Atwell, *Understanding Writing: Ways of Observing, Learning, and Teaching K–8*. Second Edition (Portsmouth, NH: Heinemann, 1988). Reprinted by permission of Heinemann Educational Books, Inc.

Page 143: From Robert Frost, *The Poetry of Robert Frost* edited by Edward Connery Lathem. Copyright © 1939, © 1967, 1969 by Holt, Rinehart and Winston. Reprinted by permission of Henry Holt and Co., Inc.

Pages 143–44: From David McCord, *One at a Time*. Copyright 1952 by David McCord. Reprinted by permission of Little, Brown and Company.

Page 144: From Karla Kuskin, *Dogs & Dragons, Trees & Dreams*. Copyright © 1980 by Karla Kuskin. Reprinted by permission of HarperCollins Publishers.

Pages 144–45: From Karla Kuskin, *Dogs & Dragons, Trees & Dreams*. Originally appeared in *Alexander Soames: His Poems*. Copyright © 1962 by Karla Kuskin. Reprinted by permission of HarperCollins Publishers.

Page 145: From Shel Silverstein, *Uncle Shelby's Zoo—Don't Bump the Glump*. Copyright 1964 by Shel Silverstein.

Page 145: From John Ciardi, *Fast and Slow*. Copyright 1975 by John Ciardi. Reprinted by permission of Houghton Mifflin Co.

Pages 154–55: From Brendan Galvin, *No Time for Good Reasons* (Pittsburgh, PA: University of Pittsburgh Press). © 1974 by Brendan Galvin. Reprinted by permission.

Page 163: From David J. Whitin, Heidi Mills, and Timothy O'Keefe, *Living and Learning Mathematics* (Portsmouth, NH: Heinemann, 1990). Reprinted by permission of Heinemann Educational Books, Inc.

Page 169: From Carl Lindner, *This Sporting Life* (Minneapolis, MN: Milkweed Editions, 1987). Reprinted by permission of Milkweed Editions.

Page 170: From Emilio De Grazia, *This Sporting Life* (Minneapolis, MN: Milkweed Editions, 1987). Reprinted by permission of Milkweed Editions.

1

poetry is for everyone

I sat by a lake, my favorite, Lake Messalonskee in Sidney, Maine. I sat in a folding chair ready to enjoy the lake's seven-mile sweep down to the small town of Belgrade, with its white steeple reaching through the trees. But within minutes the image was marred by a succession of speed boats, inboard and outboard. As my anger boiled, a poem brewed. I grabbed my notebook and wrote quickly, changing nothing, just letting the rush of words, sounds, and feelings reach the page. It took no more than fifteen minutes to get a look at what was bothering me.

SUNDAY AT THE LAKE

Deep-throated snarls,
like canines pissing
their territory on trees
the spark plugs snap
their delight, the male
bass, throttles open wide
plunge and spin racing
the wind, shattering
the thick, humid calm
of Sundays, proving Mather
right that human-kind
wants to throw sand
in the face of God . . .

That isn't where the poem ended, but the sounds I wanted got in early, as did the feeling. Above all, I had to show my anger to myself and have my own temper tantrum on paper. Later, when I reworked the poem, I decided to start it with more peaceful sounds and then have that mood broken by the noise. Here is where the beginning of the poem is at the moment:

1

SUNDAY AT THE LAKE

This quiet lake feeds
a shore of cedar, hemlock
and fir; no sound, save
cicadas and crickets,
a child at play, but now

male marauders open
throttle, their spark plugs
snapping a deep-throat
delight and like canines
pissing their territory,
spray contempt with great
gouts of bow waves gone
mad waves that slap
at kayak, canoe and sail . . .

Our lives are surrounded by poems. They come out of the mouths of friends or of small children, they are inspired by an itch, a symphony, or a repetition of sound, they record the same line spoken again and again by an impatient child or a used car salesman. Writing them down, exploring in a small space what bothers or delights us or what seems to be contradictory in our lives, gives us one of the most valuable and enjoyable tools for thought. Poetry is for us; poetry is for everyone.

I first encountered poetry in seventh grade. We had to find twenty-four poems in the library, then copy them into a personal notebook of poems and hand it in to the teacher for a grade. I remember liking Joyce Kilmer's "Trees" because it was so short and hating Edgar Allan Poe's "The Raven" because it was so long. Poetry was a standard in the curriculum. It rhymed when it was good and was to be revered, the badge of an educated person, but it had little to do with the present tense of life.

Back in the sixties Marshall McLuhan wrote, "The artist is the antenna of civilization." I think the poet as artist—the individual, whether five or sixty-five, who writes or speaks about the details of everyday living and shapes them by matching sound and sense—will develop a strong sense of self. Many of us studied poetry in college, but poets were placed in such an elite position that any notion of attempting to take the field with a few lines of our own was considered preposterous. Courses in poetry required us only to read poetry, not to write it. Poetry was a genre "on a hill."

WHAT IS POETRY? Poetry brings sound and sense together in words and lines, ordering them on the page in such a way that both the writer and reader get a different view of life. Linda Rief, a middle-school teacher in Durham, New Hampshire, writes about a porcupine she observes crossing a road:

> *Waddle and lurch*
> *Waddle and lurch*
>
> *I stop my car*
> *as the porcupine*
> *hunkers across*
> *the road.*

Some words in our language carry both the sound and the feel of the very thing they depict. Linda uses "waddle" and "lurch" to describe the motion of the porcupine. The feel of the words in the mouth carries the sense of the porcupine's motion. Then she repeats them for emphasis. In poetry the repetition of sound accentuates both image and meaning. Sometimes the sounds repeat at the end of a line, as in the first four lines of Shakespeare's Sonnet 73:

> *That time of year thou mayest in me behold*
> *When yellow leaves, or none, or few, do hang*
> *Upon those boughs which shake against the cold,*
> *Bare ruined choirs where late the sweet birds sang*

(Behold, cold; hang, sang.) Sometimes they repeat in the interior of a line, as in Shakespeare's

> *When to the sessions of sweet, silent thought*

where the repeated "s" makes a soothing sound. I tried to create that same kind of feeling in my own poem about the lake:

> no sound, save
> cicadas and crickets,
> a child at play . . .

Helen Phillips, a third-grade child in Golden, Colorado, demonstrates the same sensitivity to sound and meaning in her poem "If I were":

IF I WERE

> If I were the wind,
> I'd kiss the tops of tulips in the
> Twilight.
>
> If I were the rain, I'd
> Sprinkle the pines lightly at dusk.
>
> If I were the sun,
> I'd shine brightly on the mountains
> At noon.
>
> If I were the snow,
> I'd cover the earth with
> A soft blanket of white at
> Dawn.
>
> . . . and . . . If I were you, I'd make
> Life as wonderful as possible,
> At any time or place.

Judy Curlington Latimer, a reading teacher from Buffalo, New York, orders the lines in this poem to explore her middle years. Poems are like personal narratives in that they draw on the same types of information, but they concentrate it in a shorter space:

EMBRACING THE DARK

*Diving into
the sweet freedom
of my middle years
I learn
to accept
the loneliness
of my choices.*

*As gliding in
the silky water
of the pond
I teach myself
to feel
the spidery arms
of seaweed
as a caress.*

*Or exploring
ocean pools
between the tides
for their varied red
and yellow-green life
I don't turn my back
on the rank stagnant pool
but look
into its dark shallows
to see
what is there.*

*Or shocked
into realizing
that my daughter's
love life
has begun so soon
I invite*

the usurper
into my kitchen
and make friends.

We create poetry every day in the way we repeat sounds or use metaphor to teach, make a point, or have a good laugh. How well I remember the student in the center of a city who was asked to write a character sketch. Instead, he not only wrote a character sketch in one line but also started a poem:

When Miss Bell yelled,
everyone's ass tightened
just a little bit.

ACTIONS FOR INVOLVEMENT   The Actions in this book will involve you in both the reading and writing of poetry—for yourself, for the children, and for you and the children together. Actions describe teaching approaches to try with children. They put you in motion with experiments in learning. Many of them also provide an opportunity to read and write poetry for yourself. If you have wondered what it might be like to write poetry, here is your chance to experiment with poetry in all sorts of ways. You will begin to understand poetry from the inside because you have experienced it, and you will be able to help children as they experiment with language and poetry.

Where possible, try the Actions with a colleague so that you can share your writing and the books you read and discuss the progress in your classrooms. Even if you do not wish to try the same Actions together, you will still be able to share your experiences from writing and from the classroom.

Poetry, like music, involves an enormous range of individual taste. The Actions will invite you to experiment with reading poems aloud. Some of these you will enjoy, while other selections may strike you as closer to "hard rock" or to a Bach chamber piece. My contact with poetry, from grammar school through advanced study, has usually been one in which the literary canon was dropped on my foot with a "This is good for you because. . . ." Some of the pieces I liked, some I didn't. For some reason I always felt a little guilty when some of the "great ones" turned me off.

Since I began writing poetry myself, I have a better understanding of how poetry affects others. Few remain neutral when it comes to responding to poetry. In fact, a neutral response usually means that the listener is utterly befuddled or even politely hostile. Sometimes only one or two people like my favorite poems. Other poems I write are enjoyed by many people even though I have whisked them off quickly. Apparently they touch a more universal chord. Poetry, as it reflects the sounds, joys, sorrows, and anger in our lives, will touch parts of ourselves that bring joy as well as aspects of ourselves we simply don't like.

2

read poetry aloud

Poetry was meant to be read aloud. In fact, both prose and poetry should be read aloud more often than they are. I recall a high school teacher in East York, Ontario, who shared a story about one of his struggling black-jacketed students. The teacher, a good oral reader and a writer in his own right, had just finished reading a short story aloud to the class. The student sat staring at the floor, then with a puzzled, inquiring look on his face asked, "When you read to yourself does it sound the same way to you as when you read it aloud?"

"Not exactly the same, but yes, it does sound something like that to me, especially on certain parts," the teacher replied.

"Well, it doesn't sound like that to me at all . . . ever. I wish it could sound like that to me." The student's statement, which provides one of those rare insights into what many go through as readers, also speaks to the importance of "sound" in learning. Sound is first externalized through oral reading, in which we sense different voices and the different values words have in varying contexts. In short, we hear "outside" before we can represent sound "inside."

When I write poetry I frequently "sound" it as I compose. I am not much different from a first grader. I want to listen as the text strikes the page. I also reread aloud. When I practice with sound it also helps if I read the prose and poetry of others aloud.

ACTION: PRACTICE READING POEMS ALOUD WITH A PARTNER.

Find someone who will agree to read some poems aloud into a tape recorder and compare the reading with your own. Notice that there are several ways to read a poem depending on the way it is interpreted. The sound of the voice follows the meaning and thus interprets to others the richness of the language and the subject of the writing. The reading makes the poem sound more like conversation with some rhythm added to it.

Here are several short poems to read aloud. Read them all aloud twice, then select the one that appeals to you most for several rereadings. By several, I mean at least four or five oral readings. Each time, experiment with making the poem sound right to you.

ICICLES

Slender beads of light
hang from the ceiling.

My son shows me
their array of sizes:

one oddly shaped,
the queer curve,

a clear walrus tooth,
illumined, tinseled.

We watch crystal cones
against blue sky;

suddenly some break loose;
an echo of piano notes.

The sun argues
ice to liquid.

Tiny buds of water,
pendent on dropper tips,

push to pear shapes:
prisms that shiver silver

in a slight wind
before falling.

Look, he says laughing,
a pinocchio nose,

and grabs one
in his tiny hand,

touching the clear carrot
cold to his lips.

Mark Irwin

Since this poem has a slight narrative line, try reading it as an unfolding story. Feel the sounds the author repeats. Experiment with accentuating them (p's, c's).

IN FIRST GRADE

In first grade
everything is edible;
soft, primary pencil wood
to run my teeth down
like corn on the cob.

Second course is paste
during reading while
Miss Jones' yellow eye
and green smile catch
me in mid-mastication
of a primary chairback
during story time,
fresh erasers nipped off
the end of a borrowed pencil
or brown art gum erasers
offered as hors d'oeuvres
from the art supply cabinet;

Then I reach for the fragrant
golden ends of Delores Gallo's
hair hanging over the back
of her chair and on to the books
on my desk.

At recess rawhide webbings
in a baseball mitt, then green
crabgrass pulled just so
to gnaw white succulent stems
like salad at Sardi's.

Who needs warm milk
and graham crackers smelling

of the janitor's basement
at the Webster School
when we're already seven courses in?

Don Graves

Perhaps you recall your own gnawing habits or even observe them in students of all ages today. Experiment with different tasting voices for the various courses.

Here is an apt poem about a very common experience, the obnoxious cold. The tone is different from the rest.

COLD HEAD, COLD HEART

I suppose no one has ever died of a head cold
while not fearing or fervently
wishing to do so on the hour,
gasping through a nose the size of Detroit.

My mouth tastes of moldy sneaker.
My tongue is big as a liverwurst.
My throat steams like a sewer.
The gnome of snot has stuck a bicycle pump in
my ear.

I am a quagmire, a slithy bog.
I exude effluvia, mumbled curses,
and a dropsy of wads of paper,
handerchiefs like little leprosies.

The world is an irritant
full of friends jumping in noisy frolic.
The damned healthy: I breathe on them.
My germs are my only comfort.

Marge Piercy

Disgust sits deep in the poet's throat and pushes forth all kinds of sounds. When I read I focus on the sounds from the head and the back of the throat.

Here is another poem, which has a certain elegance in its clever rendering of a shifty man, the tricky pitcher.

PITCHER

His art is eccentricity, his aim
How not to hit the mark he seems to aim at,
His passion how to avoid the obvious,
His technique how to vary the avoidance.

The others throw to be comprehended. He
Throws to be a moment misunderstood.

Yet not too much. Not errant, arrant, wild,
But every seeming aberration willed.

Not to, yet still, still to communicate
Making the batter understand too late.

Robert Francis

ACTION: EXPERIMENT WITH A TAPE-RECORDING OF YOUR VOICE TO SEE HOW YOU INTERPRET THE TEXTS.

Choose a poem you like and read it aloud into the tape recorder. Do it for yourself first, but read it knowing that ultimately you will share the tape-recording with another person. It makes a difference to do it this way. I find that if I know I will share either the direct reading or the audio recording of my reading I do a better job of trying to interpret the poem with my voice than if I record it only for myself.

I learn to read a poem aloud the same way I learn to do successive drafts in a piece of writing. I use this approach as a general practice:

My first reading is a very rough oral interpretation. I simply read the poem, listening as I read for connections between sound and meaning. For example, when I first read "Icicles," I noticed that there was a kind of unfolding narrative to the poem, but I didn't discover that until I was a little more than halfway through. A narrative poem conveys the sense of an unfolding story: "Listen to what is coming next." "Pitcher," on the other hand, has a more essaylike flavor.

Next, I apply what I've discovered in my first reading. For example, I read "Icicles" with that sense of unfolding narrative—the story of a boy and his dad discovering icicles together. This time I'm looking for the stories, the short episodes that carry their own kind of meaning.

Now I begin to interpret with greater precision the small units of meaning I have discovered in the previous reading. At first these units are in pairs: the oddly shaped icicle, the clear walrus tooth. But I also discover longer units that go together and read them accordingly:

> *The sun argues*
> *ice to liquid.*
>
> *Tiny buds of water,*
> *pendent on dropper tips,*
>
> *push to pear shapes:*
> *prisms that shiver silver*
>
> *in a slight wind*
> *before falling.*

There is also the final unit, "Look, he says . . ." that carries the poem to the end. When I read the section "The sun argues . . ." I notice that Irwin accentuates the forming of drops through the use of "p" sounds. I find my lips puckering forward just as the drops would form at the end of icicles. Notice that successive readings carry me further and further into the details that accentuate meaning still more. Although I am demonstrating how I discover these elements in reading a poem, please know that while some of these insights may come in a first oral reading, others may not emerge until maybe years later, after reading the same poem dozens of times. That is the joy of reading poetry—the continual discovery of new meaning. When I push my voice to discover, the poem reveals itself to me more and more.

Listen to the tape and follow your reading of the poem. Note how you use your voice. Which words are you accentuating? Where are you pausing? Is your voice loud or soft? Note the line breaks, which seem to punctuate a thought that may be sustained through as many as four lines. For example, I try to hear what my voice does when I read the final stanza of "Pitcher" by Robert Francis. Again, you will find it useful to listen to the tape several times to see how various interpretations come through in different readings. Now, with a colleague, replay the tape. Discuss how well your voice supports the sense you wanted to convey in your oral interpretation.

Try for a general understanding of the text when you read. Oral interpretations go through a process similar to that of drafting a piece of writing: first, a rough cut of what the poet meant, then gradually a greater and greater precision as you focus on specific words in the text.

Every time I read a poem aloud I try to hear new meanings. In short, I try to approach it with a sense of "discovery" that may help me to take the same stance as I listen. The reading both invites and explores meaning for me. As I grow in my understanding of a poem and my appreciation of it, my rereading becomes a genuine invitation to the wonder it inspires.

ACTION: READ POETRY ALOUD TO CHILDREN.

How important it is to share poetry with children! Sharing the sound and sense of a poem can be one of the most delightful moments in your teaching day. Above all, share the poems that delight you. You will gradually gain a clearer sense of what types of poems you and the class enjoy most together.

Read poetry aloud without analyzing it or introducing vocabulary. (Of course, if someone asks about the meaning of a word, I'll respond.) Too much poetry has been ruined for children by lengthy introductions and careful directions on what they should "learn." Poets write with the intention that their poems stand alone, without extensive introductions.

This does not mean that you should not discuss poems after they have been read aloud. The discussion can follow broad guidelines: "What struck you about the poem? Did any particular words create interesting pictures? Were there any words you especially liked? What did you wonder about?" Occasionally I might ask, "What do you suppose the poet was thinking when he or she wrote the poem?" I hope there will be a broad range of interpretation and taste. I encourage differences of opinion and urge children to state specifically why they have other tastes.

3

write poetry with children

Poetry began to be a part of you when you practiced reading it aloud. You felt the impact of sound and sense. You relived the nuisance of the common cold with Marge Piercy's "Cold Head, Cold Heart." As you read Mark Irwin's "Icicles" and my "In First Grade," perhaps you saw pictures of icicles or of first-grade children chewing away on pencils, paste, and paper. Perhaps you felt sympathy or delight. You produced those images and experienced these feelings because you were actively composing a text of your own as you read. Reading, especially reading poetry, is a highly active enterprise.

I invite you now to experiment with poetry by writing some for yourself and by writing some with the children. You will discover, I suspect, that poetry is not a genre "on a hill." Rather, it is for all those who wish to write about what they care about, to relive scenes, recall images, and savor experiences that otherwise pass fleetingly through their minds. To put some of them on paper is to give meaning a very concrete form. The best part about poetry is that you can experience in a short space what sometimes takes pages and pages to experience in prose.

Poetry is first of all for you. Join me in practicing a few simple beginnings with a view to delightful experimentation. Practicing poetry for yourself will allow you to become more closely acquainted with your own thinking. Later, you can continue your learning when you write with the children. I will do the same. I will be learning right along with you as I respond to each Action, and I will share my writing with you. We will experiment together.

For each Action you try there will be a corresponding Action to try with the children. You might try these Actions with the entire class as you all begin to work with poetry together, or, if you feel more comfortable, you might start to write and teach poetry during reading/writing time with a cluster of five or six children. (If you wish to get a better overview of various options for using poetry in your classroom and in your curriculum, read Chapter 4 before you start your program.)

GETTING STARTED Most poets speak of the first rush of words. You may say, "First rush of words? Are you kidding? I'm lucky if I can come up with two words." But I say, "The words will rush out if you just let them take off and follow them without censoring. Lower your standards and just get words on the page."

Everyone has a different entry point for discovering the poems around them. I want to share a few of these here. Pick up your pen, your pencil, or whatever helps you write most rapidly. In my case, I'm most comfortable composing at my computer. I'll compose along with you to show you what I mean. I promise you that what you see here will be my first drafts.

ACTION: **EXPERIMENT WITH A LIST POEM.**

I've found that the list poem is one of the easiest ways to enter into the writing of poetry. I am grateful to Georgia Heard, author of *For the Good of the Earth and Sun*, for introducing me to this approach. Composing a list poem frees you to feel how one line triggers another. I listen to myself a little better with a list than I do when I work with a full line.

Right now I am listening to Mozart's twenty-first piano concerto. What follows is the short list poem that was triggered by the concerto.

Stately
fingers
flying
pressing
pushing
melodies
kings
courts
a child
feet
swinging

white
powdered
wig
laughter

First I felt my fingers on the computer keys playing words instead of notes. As sounds came from the keyboard, I imagined a court setting, the kind in which Mozart might have played before a king, and the words "kings" and "courts" followed. Then the child Mozart appeared, a scene perhaps from the motion picture *Amadeus*. He was short and his legs were swinging, barely able to reach the pedals of the piano. I caught a glimpse of him from the rear and noted that he was wearing a powdered white wig.

When I began my list I had no idea I would end up with a picture of Mozart himself. That's the best part of the list poem. The words go down more quickly than they do in writing full lines, and I can follow my ideas and images quite rapidly. I try to make the list as specific as possible because specificity usually allows me to see more pictures. The pictures, in turn, create an emotional response. Occasionally I'll add the emotion I am feeling to my list. Here is what might have happened in my poem if I had put down my feelings as I wrote. The added words are in roman:

Stately
fingers
flying
free
pressing
pushing
joy
melodies
kings
courts
stiff

a child
feet
swinging
white
powdered
wig
laughter
silly

I find it easier to write a list poem if I choose an object or a
situation I know will involve feelings. It is also important that
my choice produces pictures, that I see the object or the situation in my mind.

ACTION: USE A STARTER TO EXPERIMENT WITH POETRY.

In the past, giving children story starters or first lines has been
considered close to anathema. It's true that the history of teaching writing is filled with all kinds of gimmicks and assigned
topics designed to bypass children's thinking. But there are
times when a writer's diet can be enriched by experimenting
with a first line or preset situation. In addition, when children
are already choosing most of their topics and have demonstrated good, independent thinking, starters or "triggers" can
be a useful means of leading them to new ways of thinking.
Here are some triggers that can become the first lines of poems:

- I am the person who . . .
- The time is right for . . .
- She (he) went . . .
- The dog (or any animal you choose) has . . .
- The wind blows . . .
- Presidents should . . .

I'll experiment with several of those starters to see what happens. Remember, these are for you, the teacher. Although some
of them may work for children, the approaches I am suggesting

here are to help you to discover poetry and learn to listen to your own voice.

One of the easiest starters for me is the first line "I am the person who. . . ." I have a catalog of personal foibles that would reach into the hundreds. I'll write a quick draft of a poem giving as many concrete pictures of my catalog as I can. I'll change nothing as I compose on my computer. Here goes:

I AM THE PERSON

I am the person who
checks the temperature each morning,
sets the coffee for brew the night before,
a clock watcher, an efficiency nut
who measures time and space
like he'd check money in his wallet;
I am the person who worries
about the growing paunch
of older age, who diets
and exercises in weary
alternation; I am the person
who greets the dawn,
and walks zombie fashion
between 2:00 and 4:00 P.M.
I am the person who
lives Mozart, Mozart, Mozart,
piano, orchestrals, who
adores his genius;
I am the person who
reads the sports page
first, winners are always
there, next page one,
then weather and business.

That's a quick first draft. I've tried to take what I know about myself and introduce some specifics. Take ten minutes now and begin your own poem with one of the first-line starters. Write rapidly, change nothing, and let the lines flow on the page without worrying. Enjoy yourself.

I'll try another first-line starter (try this one first if it seems more natural to you):

THE TIME IS RIGHT

The time is right for the gathering
of leaves, the golds, the reds,
the radio said this was peak
day today, but I sit and write
and wonder what this one day
means when it goes by and I have
not moved from this chair
and the moment is lost
and I look back at the reds
now turned to bronze,
the yellow maples fluttering
to rest on pavement, car, and child
sitting in a carriage who sees
the precise peak moment
of the leaves, but sees only
yellow, no moment, just yellow
flutters, yellow birds to him
yellow moments to brighten his
day in a carriage when that
morning his mother yelled
at his father, heaved the cat
out the door and took him down
the lane for new air and peace
and quiet, and who cares what
the precise moment is when yellow
flutters in the sun, the lost
moments of summer shouting new
joy in the spinning cartwheels

of yellow maples saying goodbye
to summer, hello to their new child.

There it is, a fast six-minute poem on my computer, no words changed. That is the discipline; no words should be changed in a first draft. The key is to listen to the words and follow the images they create with other words. In the first four or so lines, I was just prancing in place waiting for something to trigger me off. I sat in my study, looking at my maple tree, whose leaves turn yellow every year, and remembered the radio announcer saying, "And today is the peak for leaf color." I thought, "So, what does that mean for me? Am I supposed to do something?" The first lines wondered and waited. But then the child in the carriage came in and I asked myself, "What does this mean to a child?" Well, there certainly isn't any peak moment. Then I wondered about the child's mother. Why is the child outdoors?

For me, a poem becomes a whole series of questions and answers, although most of the questions don't appear on the poem's surface, while the answers become the poem itself. I suspect that "peak for leaf color" didn't mean a thing to the mother; she just wanted to get out of the house. What, then, did "peak" mean for the leaves? For them, there was a moment, a precise moment, when bright yellow leaves became an offering to the child, who could not know of the offering yet took it in as one of those moments of joy that come in a split second. It is the child who knows. At least I think that's what's there. I didn't know that until after I'd written it. I listened and watched the scene, wrote, and learned.

I liked the first draft of my poem and came back to it. Eight drafts later it looks like this:

THE TIME IS RIGHT

The time is right
to gather the leaves,

the golds, the reds,
the radio says
today is the peak
but I sit, write
and wonder what
this one day means
when I have not moved
from this chair,
and the moment is lost
the reds turn to bronze
and the yellow leaves rest
on pavement, car and child

who sits in a stroller,
misses the moment of peak
and sees only yellow birds
to brighten his day,
when that morning his mother
yelled at his father,
heaved the cat out the door
and took him down the lane,
for new air and no noise,
but who cares about peak
when gold joy cartwheels
in the last sun of summer
to say hello to the new child?

I'll try another first-line starter, "He went . . . ," in order to see where the poem goes. All I know is that it will be about a man who goes to church, nothing more. I see a man entering a church or getting out of his car. I watch and listen—to the man, the scene, and myself:

A MAN WENT TO CHURCH

A man went to church today,
a tie carefully shaped in place,

the trousers neatly pressed,
to be ready for God, to be ready
for his mother's voice,
whispering "well done" from the graves,
from the mornings when he put
on the itchy pants in second grade,
cried the itch, the pain of sitting
on that little chair in a circle
when the boys made teachers cry
when they turned their back,
put up the flannel board,
to turn to tell them that Jesus
loved them, and the boys
had pinched Margaret Hemple
because she would cry,
and they would laugh,
and he, now a man, laughed
to know his mother would
cry too because church
was silly, a trick to make
him wear itchy pants, sit still,
grow up, but now his pants
are smooth, his smile rich,
laugher jovial and though
he doesn't pinch on Sundays,
Monday through Saturday,
he rips his customers
and makes them cry,
and on Sunday he is contrite,
smiling, and loveable.

This one didn't seem to work as well for me as the others, at least for a rapid first draft. Nevertheless, there is a person emerging in the poem I'd like to know better. I suspect that there is some link between his early Sunday school attendance and his current behavior, maybe his mother's insistence that he go. Perhaps the approval of his mother from the grave is an indication of other elements that ought to appear. I don't know. I will have to write and revise to find out. But I will enjoy the journey and the answer as it emerges from the words on the page. I did rework the lines of this poem, but I didn't like them. For me, there wasn't a poem there, or at least nothing I thought I wanted to find out.

You may wish to come up with your own first lines. Write them down and work through a quick draft, and then try writing down the questions that arise—some of the "why" questions or some of the "what" questions that will demand more detail. For example, in the last poem, I decided that the man's mother might be more interesting. I needed more specific information about her. I probably needed to describe her in writing, to feel her presence, in order to know what kind of woman would come back to him from the grave.

All these questions of why and what are rambling around in my mind, and I can't wait to see where they lead. In fact, maybe I will write for five minutes here to sketch in the mother:

> *Mrs. Pym wanted*
> *to be right,*
> *wanted the dishes,*
> *the beds, the ironing,*
> *the garden, minus all*
> *weeds, to be in straight*
> *rows, arriving at right*
> *angles to the lawn,*
> *and with her hair*
> *combed long and neat*
> *for viewing only*
> *in the afterhours*
> *when her son, Chester,*
> *had gone to bed*

and she could reflect
on his rightness
of learning, the chores
he had done, the time
not wasted, the obedience
observed, she could
tarry a look at the long,
golden hair cascading
over her shoulders,
admired by a man
ten years ago, gone
to the sea, but now
tied tightly in a bun,
and poked prissily
with forked needles
to stay just so.

The name, Mrs. Pym, was a help. The landlady who lived upstairs when I was seven years old had that name. Although I didn't have her image in mind in writing this, the name seemed right for a woman so worried about being correct. The emergence of her long, golden hair was a breakthrough for me. I was surprised by it and for a moment wondered what to do with it. It was so out of character with the woman I had described up to this point. She only allowed herself the luxury of its beauty after Chester had gone to bed. It wasn't until then that I began to understand Mrs. Pym, the woman who sent her son to Sunday school.

I liked this poem and went back to work to clarify some of the meanings that emerged in the first draft. Eight drafts later, here is where the poem now stands:

PRISCILLA PYM

Priscilla Pym rinses dishes,
tugs sheets to crisp corners,

irons apron ties to smoothness,
pulls weeds from vegetable rows
at right angles to pasture walls.

In the afterhours
when her son has gone to bed
she tastes the rightness
of his learning,
the chores completed,
the time not wasted,
the obedience observed.

She now stands alone,
to release cascades of hair
admired eight years ago
by a man called to sea,
then raises a chin,
tarries a sideways look,
and snuffs out the light.

In the morning dark
she rises to wash,
and long in habit
pokes pins in a bun
for the daylight hours.

ACTION: TRY FIRST-LINE STARTERS WITH CHILDREN.

If children are to find first lines helpful, they ought to have a
choice. They ought to be able to select the particular journey
into words they want to take. Here are some suggestions:

- An eagle flew . . .
- Tyrannosaurus rex walked . . .
- The wind blew . . .
- I am the person who . . .
- I lowered the landing gear . . .
- I tried to catch . . .

A short mini-lesson in creating opening lines on the overhead projector, chalkboard, or experience chart paper will be helpful. After you write down a few first lines, ask the children if word pictures are beginning to emerge. "What are the details that will come after your opening line?" Children usually want to focus on the action before they add details to help the reader see what is happening. Some young writers need to do the action line first and then put in the details. For others, who are usually more developmentally advanced, the details go down along with the action. I try to elicit a few details from the child who is bound by the "action line," but it often takes a while before that child sees them as necessary.

What I am more interested in is showing children how to find poems, find opening lines in their own lives rather than in my starters. Many children, however, can't find a poem until they write a few and know what to look for.

ACTION: FIND A POEM IN WORDS THAT ALREADY EXIST.

I've just picked up two boxes, one Post Natural Raisin Bran, which I've just eaten for breakfast, the other my AOSEPT solution, which I'll use to clean my contact lenses. I'm going to look for a poem in the print on the boxes and see what happens when I try to order or reorder the words.

POST NATURAL RAISIN BRAN

People prefer Post,
no sugar on the raisins
like some other raisin brans.

These big, crispy flakes
really hold up in milk.

Filled with 12 essential vitamins,
my life is fortified
for the onslaught
of devils, curses, a wandering

flu, the shouts of my neighbor,
the cacaphony of sound,
an insulator against plagues,
pestilence, advertisements,
public disgrace,
all giving crisp to my life,
so limp, soggy and needing
of the privilege of Post's
pesky, perky flakes.

I took the first five lines from the Raisin Bran box and then just let go on "fortified." "Against what?" I asked myself, and let the words take me from there, discovering a few surprises in the process. "Crisp" also set me off. I had watched an advertisement on TV a few nights before in which Gorton's was demonstrating that their fish sticks are now guaranteed to be crunchy. (In fact, the whole advertising world has noted that Americans want their food to be crunchy. Why? Another poem.)

Let's try my AOSEPT box now. I think this one will be more difficult, but I'll play around with it anyway.

AOSEPT CATALYTIC DISINFECTION SYSTEM

A simple
one cup
system
for care
of soft
contact
lenses.

Contains
no
preservatives
and thus
the potential

*for allergic reactions
is minimized.*

*My eyes, my eyes
they care, they care
with the softness
of lenses, the gentle
solutions, whole laboratories
of white-coated technicians
gossamer in thought and drift
work day and night for only
softness and gentleness
to touch my eyes and lids,
no grating, just sterile,
youthful, eye-clearing
chemicals to take me
to a new world of sight.*

As with the Post Cereal, I took the first fourteen lines from the box and then, after feeling their rhythm, I let myself go. Cleaning contact lenses is a fairly serious procedure, and the words were lined up on the box with precision. I thought I'd order them in a much shorter line, to emphasize their attempt to give an impression of systematic activity. Somewhere I caught a vision of technicians working hard to protect my eyes for me. They were working in a sterile lab trying to make the wearing and cleaning of my lenses as easy and safe as possible.

ACTION: TRY TO DISCOVER POETRY THROUGH PROSE.

Sometimes poetry can be found in highly focused prose. Prose allows us the freedom to let the words flow without having to worry about line breaks. Here is an example of prose at work. I'll write about dawn in October in fast sentences, again not changing words as I write.

I'm a sun worshipper. I said to my wife, Betty, this morning, the older I get the more I want sun. Maybe that is why people move to

Arizona, California or Florida. Anyway, I came downstairs to go to work at 5:30 A.M. and it was pitch black, not even light shadows with a hint of dawn played on the walls. I took a look to the East and couldn't even see the familiar white line on the horizon indicating the coming of dawn. Guess that must mean it will be a cloudy day. Checked the temperature and noted 32 degrees. Well, that could only mean Northwest wind for this time of year and that had to mean a clear dawn, not a cloudy one.

Well, the sun did come up and it was a blazing, no-nonsense one, the kind that lights up the leaf colors, and gives you a good feeling for the day. I guess I want sun so badly that I forget that with each passing day from June 22nd on, the sun comes up later and later. I want the sun so badly that I can't believe that I'm getting cheated day by day by that shifty dealer of a few minutes less. I'll take a look at the paper to see when it comes up. Well, on October 5th it is 6:45 A.M. Another check shows that is the same as February 13th. Heavens, the morning light is the same as dead winter. Shakes up my rhythms of light.

I'm no different than the lilies that turn their wistful heads to the light and sun, hoping for some radiance to pick them up, to make them more beautiful. Sun does that for me, I think. It gives me a pickup, fills me with optimism, that anything can be accomplished feeling.

There are a few notions in these paragraphs that I might run with in a poem. The notion that I'm being cheated by a shifty dealer, my own yearning for light, that I've forgotten how far October 5th is from June 21st, and that I want light to start my day. Why? A question can be the start of a poem. I choose a first line to begin a first draft:

> *The foggy trundle*
> *down the morning stairs,*
> *where the lamp stabs*
> *at the dark, no aid*
> *from dawn shadows,*

> no promise of immediate
> help from the June
> lift to light. October
> gives no promise,
> no aid to the dealer
> of dawn. October sun
> lurks somewhere in Iceland
> putting on its brakes
> and drifts kicking
> in the blackness
> for the scattered
> feeble lights of an Eastern
> shore, whose optimists
> scan the stygian blacks
> for the promise of tender
> light licking through
> the clotted trees,
> where pessimists sink
> down into deep chairs,
> and fumble with coffee
> cups, grumbling
> not at slow pace
> of promised light,
> but the portent
> of 7:00 A.M. bosses,
> their shouts, snaps,
> and curses that make
> blackness in sunlight.

That was just some quick wordplay with a few of the notions in the prose, which, like a writer's notebook, stirs the deep structures of thought and triggers a few metaphors and further thoughts here and there. The prose supplies the language and a general, gentle frame in which to be still more precise through the medium of poetry.

This exercise demonstrates the similarities in composing in these two genres. All writing involves listening, questioning, and wondering, asking of each line: "Who are you? What do you mean? Why is that word there?" Through questions like these we begin to listen to our own voices.

With practice, the questions I ask myself aren't even audible. Rather, they come in the guise of imbalances or itches, which I attempt to deal with in the next line of my draft, writing rapidly. I follow my wonderment where it takes me, wandering after sound that looks for sense and sense that listens for sound.

I decided I liked the "Dawn" poem and went back to work on it. I had further questions: "Who was I? Who was the optimist, pessimist? How did the dawn approach?" Five drafts later, here is the version that tried to answer some of these questions:

DAWN

I trundle down the foggy
morning stairs, to reach
through the darkness
with no aid from dawn shadows,

for the sun still lurks
in Iceland, and puts on its brakes
to drift kicking and mumbling
for the scattered lights
of the Eastern shore, where

I probe the horizon
for the tender promises
of quiet light breathing
through trees bound
to one another
by a turgid dark,

and the pessimists' lamps
stab a stygian black

> *while they guzzle to coffee*
> *grounds and clutch at the night.*

ACTION: TRY TO DISCOVER POETRY THROUGH PROSE WITH CHILDREN.

When you write with children you will probably use experience chart paper or an overhead projector. You might also write occasionally at your desk and let the children know that you write at home. Children need to see us at work, talking out loud as we demonstrate how images evolve and words flow. We talk as we write, speaking our thoughts aloud, since the process is often invisible to children. We show how we learn, not so the children will now do exactly as we do, producing one-to-one correspondences in their learning, but because if they hang around a teacher who actively demonstrates learning, they are more likely to select what is appropriate to their own understanding. The demonstration serves as a concrete reference point in mini-lessons and conferences.

I want the children to know that poems have the same sources as their other writing. Poems can be about anything within the realm of their experience and their imagination. I might take a piece of prose I have already written and use it to show how a poem might start. The prose I choose should have a fair amount of detail in it. Ideally, it will also have a certain sound as well. Here are several paragraphs I wrote about my dog, Sadie. (Graves 1990, p. 25):

I leaned into my computer, hunched over, pushed at some words, when I felt a presence to my right. The presence was slightly below my right elbow. The presence made a huffing sound and I looked. My dog Sadie, eyes slightly bulging and glazed, licking her lips and with trembles that shuddered, starting at her shoulders and working their way to her tail, only to begin again at the shoulders, seemed to be dumping on me. "What's the matter Sadie?" I asked, as if the dog could answer. She did with a slight whimper.

"What's the matter with the dog?" I yelled to my wife in the other room, not really expecting an answer. "I'm blowing up balloons for the party tonight and one of them just broke." "Ah," I thought, "same old deal. Gunshots, or anything resembling them, set her off." But why does she plead with me? What does she expect me to do? Hold her, make them go away? I wonder.

I look the text over for some specifics, something I can see. For me, it is the sight of something, the sense of an image, that triggers a poem. When I see it, I say to myself, "What does that mean?" I'll start with Sadie's appearance. I even feel the hint of a title: "Dog Talk."

DOG TALK

Her eyes bulged,
glazed as if a friend
had died,
some awful moment
from her past
had burst to the surface,
and in the licking of lips,
and the trembles, the shudders,
that rolled and cascaded
from head to tail,
as if she'd just read
Stephen King, the lights
had gone out and she
was alone, and expected
me to turn them on again,
say it was all right,
that the world was in one piece
again; the moment called
for touching, the pat, the soft
word that made it all right,

for her to go on
in a dog's world.

I start with the dog's face, trying to show the dog's terror, and then wonder about what I'm seeing. As I visualize the details, I wonder, and I write the wonder right into the poem. The difference between this and prose is the way I compress the words and line them up, listening for sounds that carry meaning ahead. If I can, I try in the first draft to have strong, vivid words to end a line. Here are some I notice: bulged, died, shudders, cascaded. The nouns help too: lights, tail, lips, friend. I notice that the next to last line ends with a preposition, on.

After sharing the poem with my colleague, Jane Hansen, I realized that the last two lines are superfluous. I'm trying to tell you what I have already shown you. In another draft I'd take them out. These aren't rules I'm citing, just general guidelines. Notice that the discussion of writing a poem isn't that much different from the discussion of writing a piece in prose. The difference is in sound, line, length, and sense.

Ask the children to look in their folders for the parts of their pieces in which the words create pictures. Or, if the words don't create pictures but children like the potential of a scene, they can work first to add specifics, and then go on from there to decide how they wish to arrange the lines on the page.

ACTION: **FIND A POEM IN YOUR CHILDHOOD.**

My childhood is a treasury of source material for poems. I write to understand, to discover the details of my early years in order to see myself more clearly today. Sometimes I write to reexperience the delight of certain moments. I search for sources. I explore with delight, anticipating what I might find.

A few months ago I ran across my Aunt Alyce's collection of family photos. I was in some of the photos I had never seen before, and some were so startling I launched into an immediate exploration of what might be behind the eyes of the child in the photograph. One photo showed me at three years of age sitting on the grass holding two small puppies, one in either hand. Here is the poem I wrote about the photos after several drafts:

> *My fingers fondle*
> *puppy fur*
> *the softness of quiet possibility;*
> *a thought rises*
>
>   *an eagle*
> *on a sudden thermal,*
> *that disappears into a cloud*
> *shaped like the* Normandie,
> *pride of the French line.*
> *I stand*
>
>   *on the bridge*
> *where salt spray slaps*
> *my face and I command*
> *the quartermaster*
> *to change course;*
> *the briny smell*
>
>   *of low tide*
> *with Grandfather*
> *where we laugh*
> *at fiddler crabs*
> *running for their holes*
> *like an army in retreat;*
> *I look*
>
>   *up to the sun*
> *that warms my back*
> *and catch the flicker*
> *of his smile*
> *that holds my hand.*

I started with the picture of myself in the photo and the poem took off in a series of overlapping images and incidents. I was such a dreamer as a child. I can still hear my parents' voices, "Donald, wake up. What are you thinking?" From as early as I can remember, I'd be staring out the window or off into space. I saw that same look in my childhood photo.

The line breaks show how my thoughts overlapped as I went from eagles, to the *Normandie*, to walking with my grandfather.

> *a thought rises*
>
> *an eagle*
> *on a sudden thermal . . .*
>
> *of low tide*

You might want to rummage through some childhood photos to discover where your own trigger question might lie. When I write I use the details of the photo, and wait for the poem to emerge from those very details.

Other poems may reside in other objects and collections:

- A childhood toy.
- A memory of a story.
- A question from your own child.
- A gift from a parent or grandparent that you still possess today.

ACTION: TRY SOME MEMORY WORK WITH CHILDREN.

This is an option you may wish to try with a small group of interested children. Perhaps you have demonstrated your own use of a photo with the group, actually composing the poem on the spot. Or you may have written the poem from the photo and brought it to school to use in the poetry group.

Ask the children to bring in a photo of themselves at an age of interest to them. It may be easier for them to write from the photo if they can remember the circumstances of the picture. Perhaps the photo shows them demonstrating a particular feeling. In some cases, children may want to ask their parents about what was going on at the time of the photo if they can't remember.

Children may also have old toys they no longer play with that still have important memories for them. Ask them to bring in the toy or another object that has significance for them. For example, a sweater they no longer wear may trigger scenes of places or incidents when they wore the sweater.

ACTION: HELP CHILDREN BECOME AWARE OF THEIR EMOTIONS.

Children experience emotions throughout the school day and in their lives outside of school. Discovering that poetry is a means of expressing themselves helps connect literacy with everyday living. That is the main objective of this Action. Thus, this Action isn't intended to inspire a sudden all-class session on writing about emotions. On the other hand, there are a number of things you can do to help children work with their emotions through poetry.

- Become aware of classroom emotions—sorrow and sadness, happiness, boredom, anger, wonder, joy, bewilderment— and the incidents that spark them. Keep a one-day journal of emotions. Note when they occur. I may have a group session in which I simply ask, "What are the many different kinds of feelings you've felt today?" (or, if not today, on another day).
- Help children to be aware of their emotions when they occur. Don't tell them when they should feel them. Elicit a list from them. For example, show that anger is a legitimate emotion worth writing about.
- When the time is right for you, write an angry poem and share it with the class. Show where the anger came from. Over time, try to show that various emotions can result in entirely different outcomes. For example, if a child is in the middle of an emotionally charged situation, I may say,

"You've got some options for writing about the way you are feeling" (but I have to know the child well to make that statement).

The following poem had a very different outcome than my poem "Sunday at the Lake" (see Chapter 1). Deer flies are pretty common in New Hampshire on hot, humid summer days. I am a man with a bald head and deer flies are particularly obnoxious because they attack me from the rear. One day I said to myself, "I'll get back at the devils by writing a poem." The poem had a slightly serious bent at first, and then I realized how silly my notion was and switched into playing with a World War II metaphor of kamikaze flyers bombing the deck of an aircraft carrier.

DEER FLIES

Bald-headed men
are an endangered species
in the land of deer flies
square tails
or whatever damn fool name
you'd care to give them.

Kamikazes flying
out of the sun,
expendable warriors
from nature's nether larder,
they buzz in practiced formation
to bomb the open shining deck.

Death and glory
for the emperor,
wave upon wave they come,
their lethal charges
jettisoned
one by one
on the burning

*pique
below.*

Humor was possible *after* the event. If someone had asked me to write a poem *during* or *near* the event, I suspect I either couldn't have done it or wouldn't have wanted to, because the occasion was simply too unpleasant.

I want children to have a sense of occasion about emotion. The literate life constantly relates the everyday to the literate event. Poetry is a means of experiencing life as more than facts. We feel with our whole bodies what our minds say is or is not fact. Thus, our words in poetry are carefully selected, arranged for sound and sense so that the experience of writing and reading the poem becomes larger than the event or thought itself. Emotion and passion are the force behind the words. They help paint the picture that is a surprise to both writer and reader. I write in order to be surprised, to discover something new around the corner of hazy thought.

Back to occasions. I try to demonstrate occasions for writing poetry that cover a wide range of emotions and raise a lot of questions. The following are some examples I have collected as occasions for my own writing and suggestions for children:

- *Anger:*
  Self:
  The continued use of styrofoam cups.
  Our failure to listen to one another.
  Failure to support schools.
  At myself: I keep misplacing my car keys.
  Observation of emotion in children:
  I can't seem to write. Why can't I?
  I didn't get picked for the team.
  Our team lost and it wasn't fair. A bad call by the referee.
  I didn't get a turn to share my reading.

- *Sorrow and Sadness:*
  Self:
  I remember when my dog died.
  I'm sorry that my friend moved away.
  I'm sorry that this Christmas will not go well for a friend of mine.
  Observation of emotion in children:
  Death of any pet, parent, or relative.
  Loss of a friend who is no longer a friend.
  An illness, a feeling of being behind in work.
  Not doing well on a test.
  We thought there was going to be a blizzard but it didn't happen.
  I have a new baby sister.
- *Joy, thankfulness, and celebration:*
  Self:
  At last I've found the book I wanted.
  Spring is here. The tree buds are showing tiny sprigs of green at the tips.
  After three days of being sick, I'm glad to be back.
  Observation of emotion in children:
  Friends again!
  They found my dog.
  I have a new baby sister.
  I was the first to be picked.
  I got the part in the play.
  My mother is coming home from the hospital.
- *Boredom:*
  Self:
  I have all this writing to do on reports.
  I get bored with trying to keep this classroom clean.
  No experiments. People just keep doing the same old thing.
  I don't like some of the same old chores at my house.

Observation of emotion in children:
Revision is boring.
Correcting spelling is boring.
Waiting in line is boring.
Rainy, cloudy days and staying inside for a week are
    boring.
No TV is boring.

- ***A sense of wonder:***
Self:
I saw a blue heron fly over the road and into the marsh.
Look at the intricacy of the petals on this fuschia.
Look at the way the sun's rays show through the clouds.
I wonder how forks got designed this way.
I wonder why my computer won't work.
Can trees feel?
Observation of emotion in children:
Look at this toad, pollywog, snake!
See this jet (toy); it can go fast.
Look at the ice on the window. It makes funny pictures.
I see a boat in that cloud.
Mike can make a sound like a turkey.
Alison has a new ring from her grandmother. Put it in the
    sunlight, Alison.
I wonder how this story will end.

Poems are born out of questions and a wide range of emotions. When I write poems and point out the emotions and the questions that preceded them, I am not trying to reveal startling personal secrets or areas of my life that are inappropriate to share with children. I am not trying to place children in the role of confessor. Nevertheless, I do think it is important to share myself and what strikes me in the world I live in. What I share is genuine. I do not manufacture sadness or joy for the sake of teaching—or for anything else.

When I observe an emotion in a child I'll confirm what I see or ask the child if I have observed correctly. "That upsets you, John. Did I get that right?" Sensing that the feeling is strong or puzzling for the child, I may say, "There might be a poem there, John. What do you think?" Beware of making emotions a too frequent occasion for nudging children into poetry. Remember, poetry is only one genre for expression, and one genre among many, that children use on a given day in your classroom. The genre has to fit the child and the situation.

FINAL REFLECTION   In this chapter you've continued your involvement with poetry—from reading aloud to writing poems and to helping children get started writing poetry themselves. Our entire approach has been to discover poetry for ourselves and then to invite children to join us in exploring the genre with which we are all beginning to get acquainted. The Actions didn't take much time. Each of the poems you tried took about ten to fifteen minutes each—from working with first lines, discovering poems, and working with prose, to experimenting with memories from home photos.

You may have chosen to revise some of your poems, although that was not an expectation in this chapter. For both you and the children the objective was to get involved, experiment, begin to learn to listen to yourself, and begin to be acquainted with your senses, images, and emotions.

Chapter 3 focused on entering the world of poetry. Chapter 4 will help you to focus on a poetry program for your classroom. Since poetry is a way of thinking about the world in a short space, poetry becomes an important genre for children who wish to continue with it. And it is a genre that belongs throughout the curriculum.

Chapter 7 will help you continue to experiment with poetry, an essential element in advancing the quality of your own thinking. It will help you move beyond the starting point and on to different ways of becoming better acquainted with your own way of seeing and your own voice.

4

respond to children's poetry

You and the children have now read and written poetry. In the last chapter you focused on the flow of words in poetry. The children tried list poems, first-line starters, and looking for poems in prose. You may have responded informally to their work. In this chapter you will experiment with various elements in poetry that will help you identify and encourage children's potential as writers of poetry. As you develop your ability to discover what children can do, you will also discover your own potential as a teacher of poetry. In addition, you will nudge children to experiment with elements that will develop their skills as writers. Sometimes nudging children to add specifics, for example, will enable them to reveal their potential knowledge of a subject.

This chapter, along with Chapter 5, "Poetry Mini-Lessons," will help you to develop in a more systematic fashion children's skills in reading and writing poetry. Children who write poetry and understand the various elements that make good poems read the work of others differently.

Some of you may wish to get a sense of how other teachers set up their poetry programs. If you know that you work best when you can review various ways of organizing and using class time, skip ahead to Chapter 6, "Three Teachers."

Now I invite you to experiment with your teaching by spending ten minutes each day on a particular aspect of poetry. For example, you might choose to focus on verbs. This means you would circulate around the room looking for strong verbs in children's poems. A child may only have one strong verb among a number of very general verbs (have, has, was, saw). Focus on the strong verb. "I see that you have a strong verb here, in your line '*sprinted* to the corner.' That verb, 'sprinted,' carries such a fast-moving picture of your brother." Noticing and acknowledging *sprinted*, will help the child see where his potential for writing poetry might lie.

Read over the following Actions and decide which one you

will focus on first in your classroom. Then try one every day until you feel they are part of your repertoire.

- Focus on specifics.
- Focus on passion and wonder.
- Look for strong verbs.
- Look for a sense of play in composing.
- Look for the common made uncommon.
- Look for combinations of sound and sense.
- Look for metaphor.
- Practice longer conferences.

There is a great deal of overlap between one element and another. It may be enough for children to work on just *one* of these to enter into the world of poetry. And when you focus on one of these elements each day you will acquire a specific sense of what the children can do.

When I try these Actions I speak aloud to the children as I discover poetic elements within them and within their work.

- "I see you have a nice sound repetition here."
- "You care about this. I see in your struggle to get this down that you really want to say something about your dog."
- "I never would have thought about that in the same way you did, just the way you saw the sun rise."
- "I see the horse standing there but then he ran off. I'd like to see her running. How did she run? Try showing that for about five minutes on this piece of paper."

One part of sensing children's potential is gently pushing them a little farther than their most recent writing has gone. Sometimes a child's potential may lie beyond what is obvious in the words she has already written. I carry small half-sheets of 8½-by-11-inch paper with me and I leave a sheet with the child at the end of our brief conference. I might say, "Take this nudge paper and experiment for about five minutes on how you will show your cat playing with the yarn. You may not want to use it in your poem, but experiment with it anyway."

Although all children may not write poetry immediately, they possess the power to write poetry. Every child can write poetry in some form. Indeed, in the course of a day or a week every child utters lines and lines of poetry, although they may not be written down on paper. One of the elements that marks us as human is this ability to transform events, to play with language, to enjoy connections between sound and sense, and to feel passionately about the issues in our lives that are important to us.

ACTION: FOCUS ON SPECIFICS.

Poetry is not a general statement about feelings. Rather, it is rooted in the sharp images and details of everyday living that inspire feelings. The details writers use help me to stand where they have stood and feel as they would have me feel. The poet Eamon Grennan (1989) writes about taking his son to school on his first day. In two wonderful lines he captures a father's feeling for his son as he observes his son offering purple dahlias to the teacher.

> *Shyly he offers them up to her.*
> *Distracted she holds them upside down.*

Jessica has included one notable detail in her poem that shows her potential as a writer.

> *My cat is funny.*
> *She is sad too.*
> *She digs her claws*
> *into the furniture.*
> *She is mad.*
> *She is glad.*

Jessica plays with a rhyme scheme and mentions feelings but without using details that would release the same feelings in the reader. At the same time, the lines "digs her claws / into the furniture" helps me to see her cat. I'll tell Jessica how this image creates a picture for me.

I might nudge her in the following way:

TEACHER: Jessica, I see in your first line here that your cat is funny. Tell me about a time when she was funny.

JESSICA: Well, she plays with my feet under the covers.

TEACHER: Now I see why she is funny, Jessica. In fact, now I see in the same way you showed me how she digs her claws into the furniture. Poets are always experimenting. Take this piece of paper and see how your part about the cat playing with your toes would look in words on your page. You may not want to use it, but put it down as the first line, then "digs her claws" as the second. Experiment.

ACTION: FOCUS ON PASSION AND WONDER.

Roger has no words on his paper. He taps the desk with his pencil and sulks. "What's the matter, Roger?" I ask.

"There's this fire, a big fire, over by the lake. Really took off. You should have seen the flames. Way up. My Dad took me. Once a tree exploded. The whole top went bang. All flames."

"Roger, I see it." By now Roger's eyes are ablaze with the light of his own story. "You have a line there in the explosion, Roger. You have a beginning. 'A tree exploded. Bang.' Start there."

Blocking is a sign of passion. The child has something to say but doesn't know where to begin. Caring so much is enough to create a block.

There are many other signs of passion. Ask children where a poem has come from. Their words may show how much they care about the event, the person, or the animal, or just the writing of the poem itself. I look for emotion and try to help the child give life to that emotion.

Sometimes I hear children question the origin or fairness of things. If I sense that the question is there but unstated I might ask, "Why do you think that happened? Is that something that happens often? Is that fair?"

I work through questions and discussion. Only occasionally do I bring in nudge paper. I try to keep the child in touch with the big question that may have moved the child to write the poem. If the question isn't there, I may try to elicit one: "Roger, I see you are writing about the fire down by the lake. I sensed you were caught up by the beauty and excitement of that tree exploding, yet you were also worried about where the fire might go. What does that make you wonder about?"

The child may simply say, "I don't know." I asked this question because I saw a possible paradox in his recounting of the fire story. Paradox often leads to larger questions. I may not know if the child senses the paradox. I may say, "This [pointing to the poem] makes you wonder, doesn't it?" I simply wait to see if the child raises a larger question. If not, I move on. When I demonstrate writing poetry with my own poems in class, I continually speak about the larger questions, the life questions, that go along with my writing. The "big question" cannot be forced. More often than not it is revealed through the conference or through our own demonstrations.

ACTION: LOOK FOR STRONG VERBS.

The verb is one of the most useful indices of a child's writing potential. It is one of the most difficult parts of speech to use with skill and precision. Without strong verbs it is hard to move material from A to B, get on with the story, or retrieve our feelings about an occasion. The verb puts ideas in motion. An entire scene may be contained in a verb.

Today I move around the room glancing at children's poetry. On other days, and when children have chosen to write in other genres, I might find poems in their writing and remind them that they have the beginning of a poem in a verb. I also look for verbs in what the children say about their topics. For example, when Roger said the tree *exploded* I saw a poem in his use of the word. Jessica's use of the word *digs* to show what her cat did to the furniture is also the kernel of a poem.

The texts of inexperienced writers are filled with helping verbs and such colorless verbs as *get, went, saw, made*. When I deliberately look for more concrete verbs I make discoveries about children's potential that would otherwise elude me and the child. The verb is also a prime place to display passion and emotion. Helen Phillips, a third grader from Golden, Colorado, uses verbs carefully in her poem about a gypsy. Follow the poem through the verbs in roman:

THE GYPSY

Her earrings jangling, tinkling,
A babe against her chest,
She scrambled *after the caravan*
With hope and full of zest.

Her eyes did sparkle,
The babe didn't cry
As she ran *after the caravan*
Under the night sky.

She smiled *proudly*
Her head held *high,*
Her voice soared,
To reach *the caravan she must* try.

She's been left *behind*
While sleeping *on the moss,*
The others had been *mean,*
She'd make *them* pay *for her loss.*

Nudge paper is particularly important in helping children to be more colorful with their verbs. I especially look for verbs that convey little imagery. In Mark's poem, some verbs (in roman) need nudging:

THE WRECK

The car hit *the rail*
went *down the bank,*
and the man climbed *out.*
He was *okay.*
The wrecker came
and took *the car away.*

In a conference, the teacher nudges Mark to help him with his verbs. She listens carefully to the verbs he uses in his speech to help him with his written language.

TEACHER: Mark, I get a rough picture of what happened with the man. He climbed out of the car. Maybe he came out through the window. I'm not sure. But I was wondering about some of the other things that happened. You said the car hit the rail. Can you tell me more about that or what actually happened?

MARK: Well, the car hit some ice and skidded left and hit the rail and then shot right and rolled down the bank.

TEACHER: Stop right there, Mark. Already you've given me some good verbs, words that show more clearly what actually happened. I've written some of them on this piece of paper here: *skidded, shot, rolled.* I'd like you to take these and experiment with putting them into your poem. When you used them in your account of the accident, I had a clearer picture of what happened than when I first read your poem. See if you want to use them after you've experimented here on this piece of paper.

ACTION: LOOK FOR A SENSE OF PLAY IN COMPOSING.

Today I will look for children who play with words, who enjoy transforming events to their own ends. Play can be a repetitive, perseverative act without any transformations. I see transforming play in the child who takes blocks and turns them into jets, castles, and prehistoric monsters. I also see it in the child who puts on her mother's hat and becomes the adult who shops at the mall. The child sees the world as changing and, even more important, sees herself as the agent of change. Kara Oliveto, a second-grade child in Moultonborough, New Hampshire, shows her sensitivity to a changing world in her poem "In a Puddle."

> *In a puddle*
> *shadows of trees,*
> *sun and everything.*
> *Throw a rock in*
> *and see the trees, sun*
> *and everything*
> *boogie-dance!*
> *The end.*

Sometimes I can tell which children play at their writing by just observing them at work. I observe their faces and their actions, which reflect their absorption in their moments of transformation. Play is much easier to observe in very young children aged five through eight, since the action on the page is reflected in their faces. For older children, play is more frequently enacted on the page itself—in crossed-out words, lines inserted, separate drafts. When I listen to these children I hear them speak of options and new directions for their ideas. A sense of having options is often the prelude to the transforming event.

Nudging doesn't have much place in helping children demonstrate more playfulness as they compose. Rather, my role is to encourage the conditions that allow children to keep their work open-ended and help them listen to themselves in their texts. Children need time to work on their poems. Sometimes I unwittingly suggest deadlines in ways I am not aware. For example, if I ask children to write a quick ten-minute poem, I am not suggesting that the poem is "over" in ten minutes. I need to reassure them that the ten minutes is just to get into the poem; I then remind them that they have as much time as they need to complete the poem.

ACTION: LOOK FOR THE COMMON MADE UNCOMMON.

Some children have the natural urge to fuss or play with words. Their playing makes the common become uncommon. Poets are open to different ways of seeing the world and use language to reflect that uncommonness. For this reason, they guard against clichés, the too-familiar everyday ways of speaking about events.

The ability to take another point of view is in itself a kind of transforming event that often leads to seeing a common event in an uncommon way. I remember overhearing a kindergarten child chatting with another child during a field trip in a local park. She said, "We took off our shoes and walked across the brook. And the stones didn't mind us stepping on them." Very young children are used to transforming events and find poetry a natural genre for expression.

Poets are open to different points of view. They constantly ask and respond to questions in the lines of their poems. The questions arise as they try on other points of view.

When I write, I become the subject of the poem. I become the woman who is upset about war, or the Vietnam veteran who is angry. I become a stone, a fork, or a razor during shaving. To nudge children I ask "How come?" and "Why?":

• Show me how the dog looks at the boy. Show me how he feels.
• There were birds and animals in that forest fire. What about them? How would they look at the fire?

I ask questions, but it is up to the child to recognize whether the questions are worth considering. I have confidence that children will use what is helpful, if not on the spot then in other poems written several weeks later.

ACTION: LOOK FOR COMBINATIONS OF SOUND AND SENSE.

Children have a natural way of playing with sound and sense. Sometimes the sound takes precedence over the sense. The repetition of sound through rhymes, interjections, and recurring lines is pleasurable to them. The more you read poetry aloud and involve children in choral speaking, the more you will see them experiment with sound and sense when they write poetry.

As I move around the room today I am looking for alliteration that combines sound and sense. Note what I mean by alliteration:

> *racing rabbits*
> *brimming brooks*
> *big bad bears*

Some children experiment with the literal sound of an event, as Kristine Crawford does in a poem she wrote in Margaret Pelczar's first-grade classroom in Moultonboro, New Hampshire (see Figure 4–1).

Just recently I visited Nancie Atwell's school, The Center for Teaching and Learning, in Edgecomb, Maine. It was August and the children had long since finished their year, but on the easel was a poem composed on the last day of school by Abraham Stimson, a six-year-old in first grade. I was struck by the rhythm, the sense of play with words, and the repeating sounds:

> *ABOVE THE SEA AND BELOW THE SEA*
>
> *Above the sea there is*
> *A boat that sails,*
> *Below the sea there are*
> *Fish and whales,*

FIGURE 4–1   KRISTINE'S USE OF LITERAL SOUND IN A POEM

Rain

Drip Top Dotidy hop!
The rain is coming near.

Drip Top Dotidy hop!
The rain is coming near.

Sploddity Stop!
The rain is here
and give me a frightening
(thunder)   (lightening)

When it comes to .
                                    (lightening)

And above the sea is
A storm that hails.

You know above the sea,
It is hailing—
Below the sea,
It is "whaling"
Because the whale is
Eating the fish,
The fish is
Swimming in the water.

The water is
Holding the boat
The boat is
Catching the whales.
It goes on and on
And never ends.
And so—
Good-bye!

"Did Abraham dictate that poem?" I asked, not quite believing a six-year-old could compose such a poem.

"No," Nancie replied. "His teacher, Susan Stires, saw it in prose and recognized that it was in fact a poem and helped him to line it off. But, there is more here than meets the eye. Abraham put so much of our year's study of whales, the sea, boats, and weather into the poem as well. He may write this way because every single day, for 180 days, we end the day with a poem."

There are many more elements I could look for in my walk through the classroom to unveil the poets within the children. Metaphor, simile, and assonance are only a few of them. Again, my purpose in moving around the room, taking five to ten minutes each day to focus on one element, is to discover for myself and for the children their potential as poets. I teach best when I have that rich sense of possibility.

ACTION: LOOK FOR METAPHOR.

Metaphors allow us to avoid the clichés of the everyday and see and experience the ordinary afresh. I recall interviews Ruth Hubbard conducted with first-grade children while asking them about how they thought. One child said, "Well, I hit rewind, then I hit forward, and when I come to what I want to say or write, I hit stop." The child chose a tape recorder as a metaphor for thought. In one sense Ruth's question provided a natural opportunity for metaphor, since the nature of thought is unseen. The child created a metaphor, something Ruth knew and could see, to explain the unseen.

To bring out metaphor I might have asked Roger about the forest fire he witnessed with his father:

DON: Roger, when you stood there and saw that tree explode, what was it like? [*Asking what something is like moves into metaphorical territory.*]

ROGER: Oh, hmmmm, it was like a . . . like a . . . a bomb went off, or like one of those things on TV where a car goes bang and a big ball of fire goes up.

DON: Now I see it more clearly. I've seen both of those, the bomb and the car. I feel it too. Try experimenting on this piece of paper to show what the explosion was like. Say it again.

ROGER: When the fire got hot, the top of the tree exploded like a bomb.

DON: Good, write that down here on this piece of paper, then experiment with where you'd put it. You may not use it, but experiment for a while and tell me what you think.

If Roger uses it in his poem I'll go further into the nature of metaphor, showing him how he has put two things together, the tree on fire and the bomb. I'll also show him how other authors have used the device to help us understand and feel as the author must have felt.

When I write with the class I may point out where I have already used metaphor. My hunch here is that I'd seldom say to the class, "Now I think I need a metaphor. Let me see what I'd do." I find that the use of metaphor is overworked. That is, there is such an emphasis on it in schools that the poem exists for the metaphor rather than the metaphor for the poem. It becomes a device that shows you are a poet. My hope is to help the child to play with language. The metaphor is one more way in which to transform experience.

ACTION: PRACTICE LONGER CONFERENCES.

Not all conferences lend themselves to the quick nudge. Sometimes more listening is required. After trying the Actions that help you to sense poetic potential in the children and the short conferences with nudges, move into some longer conferences. Shorter conferences are better, but there are times when more help is needed.

Poetry is meant to be spoken or read aloud. When I respond to a child's poem, I usually ask the child to read it aloud. I want the child to hear the sound and sense of it while I hear how the child values the words. Afterwards I'll ask the child what sounds or parts seemed more important. Then I'll tell the child what I heard. Poems move ahead on the specifics, whose value shows in the way the writer expresses the words when they are read aloud.

I push for the details that make the pictures that carry the sense. Consider the following poem:

SPRING

It is spring;
the sun is out
the birds sing
we go on the swing,
I want to have a fling.

This is rather typical of the poems young children compose when the rhyme scheme dominates. To this child poetry requires rhyme. Sense takes a back seat. But the child is just beginning to write poetry, and I treat her efforts to write a poem as sincere.

TEACHER: Would you read this poem aloud to me, Karen? [*Karen reads the poem aloud and I listen to what seems to be important to her in the piece. She hits the rhyming scheme hard, accentuating the last word in each line.*]

KAREN: I couldn't think of a word to rhyme with spring when I wrote the second line. All I could think of was "the sun is out." Should I take it [the line] out?

TEACHER: Sounds mean a lot to you, Karen. I can see that. You worked hard to get them in. I was wondering what you wanted the reader to understand after reading your poem, or what you wanted the reader to feel.

KAREN: I don't know. I just wanted to write about spring, that's all.

TEACHER: Okay, I asked because you don't always have to rhyme in poems. Sometimes it is easier to write if you just concentrate on meaning, like in Karla Kuskin's poem "Around and Around" we read the other day. In the other one we read, "The Meal," she did use rhymes. You might want to experiment with writing this same poem without worrying about rhyme.

KAREN: I think I'll keep it like it is.

TEACHER: All right, this is the way you want it for now. Thank you for reading the poem to me.

My timing may have been off, or perhaps Karen wasn't ready to accept the option of writing without a rhyme scheme. But her response lets me know that I will need to accentuate non-rhyming poems in my own demonstrations and in the poetry I share in class. Rhyme schemes and sound are important, but when they dominate meaning in children's poems, the children need help.

If I think a child can handle more direction I may say, "I'd like you to take about ten minutes and write this without worrying about rhyme. Here is some nudge paper on which you can experiment." I may offer some help with specifics to encourage the child to use crisper images. "What's it like when the sun is out? Like when the sun hits a tree or anything else you want to show about the effect of the sun. Look out the classroom window; what do you see? When you show me the effect of the sun, then I appreciate the need of the sun for your poem."

Here is another poem in which a young writer, in this case, twelve-year-old Amanda, uses poetry to share her feelings, and she works very hard to do so. But the feelings are just feelings if I don't know what triggers them. Thus, as a reader, I cannot participate in what is obviously very painful to her.

> *THE DREGS*
> *Sometimes I feel so down,*
> *the aches inside hurt,*
> *and I keep going*
> *until the tears*
> *roll over me like*
> *some wave and nobody*
> *knows how much pain*
> *there is and I just*
> *don't feel like doing*
> *anything at all.*

Poems of this kind are often written by young adolescents, who are describing inner feelings for the first time. Words like "aches," "tears," "pain" are intended to move the reader. But as a reader, I have a problem; I don't know what is causing the pain and therefore I can't participate in what the writer wants me to feel.

I want to be sensitive to Amanda's purposes during our conference. It may be that she is writing for herself and does not wish to put in the details of her pain. I also recognize that first attempts to deal with feelings are usually quite global. The writer does not realize that the details are not present or that the reader needs them in order to understand the poem.

TEACHER: How's it going, Amanda?

AMANDA: Pretty good. I've got a new poem here.

TEACHER: Like to read it?

AMANDA: No, you read it. Here. [*The way Amanda gives me the poem it is clear she doesn't want it read aloud. She knows I often ask students to read poetry aloud.*]

TEACHER: Quite a title, "The Dregs." Sounds like you were pretty down when you wrote this. That right?

AMANDA: I'd just had it with things at the house. My mother keeps working on me. Then, we are going to move from here.

TEACHER: Have you written poems like this before, Amanda? I mean, have you written a poem where you said in words how you actually felt?

AMANDA: No, I haven't. Took me a while to decide to write this.

TEACHER: Then that is an important first step. Quite an act of courage to finally take a pen and put this down. It helped me to know the source of it, your mother working on you and that you were moving away. That's hard to take. Some day you might want to put that information in here. It takes time to think it over.

I don't want to minimize Amanda's first step in writing a poem about inner feelings. Although the specifics aren't there, some of them did come out during the conference. Later, I may be able to encourage her to bring in some details about those feelings, for her sake and the reader's. We often say that the reader needs details. Actually, the writer, as first reader, needs them even more. Until I actually use the details of an experience in my own writing, I don't know much more than the reader. I only have a generalized feeling of pain. But when I add the details, the pain may lessen or get worse depending on how words reveal the actual truth of the matter. If Amanda were to put in details to clarify her situation, she might have revised in the following way:

THE DREGS

The voice harps
from the first floor,
"Cleaned your room yet,
done the laundry?"
"Seems like you're
never here . . ."
and like a saw blade
that cuts in
chewing away on my backbone
until I feel
so weak I run
to my room
soaking up pillows
and thinking about friends
I'll leave and they'll leave
a hollow and their voices
that comfort and listen
will fade and only the voice
with a knife in it
will be left in the air.

Choose some children with whom you will have a more lengthy conference. By lengthy, I mean more time than you used in your conferences to understand writer potential and longer than the "nudge" type. Your first attempts may last for five to seven minutes; with experience, you will be able to reduce them to two to four minutes.

If this type of conference is new to you, choose a child you've found receptive to help in the past. Remember, poetry conferences are no different from other writing conferences:

- Let the child do most of the talking.
- Listen for the child's intentions.
- Work for flow and details.
- Let most of the skills be handled during mini-lessons (see Chapter 5).
- Help the child to keep in touch with her progress.

FINAL REFLECTION   As a teacher, you have an active role to play in helping poetry become part of children's lives. Every child has the potential to write poetry. It is not a genre for a select few. The world of poetry helps us to see that life is about more than facts. In the short space of a poem we can explore the important meaning behind events. Poetry is important to our enjoyment and sound thinking.

It takes time to search for the poet in every child. Now you have made yourself sensitive to the factors to look for. Children who write with specific details and images and use strong, interesting verbs, who tell what they know about a subject that means something to them, have already made a good start.

Chapter 5, "Poetry Mini-Lessons," builds on your responses to children in Chapter 4. Now you have a sense of their potential as well as of the effects of your nudging. You are more aware of your own knowledge of teaching poetry because you have read and written poetry with the children. Mini-lessons are more formal attempts to follow up on the specific teaching a number of children need at one time.

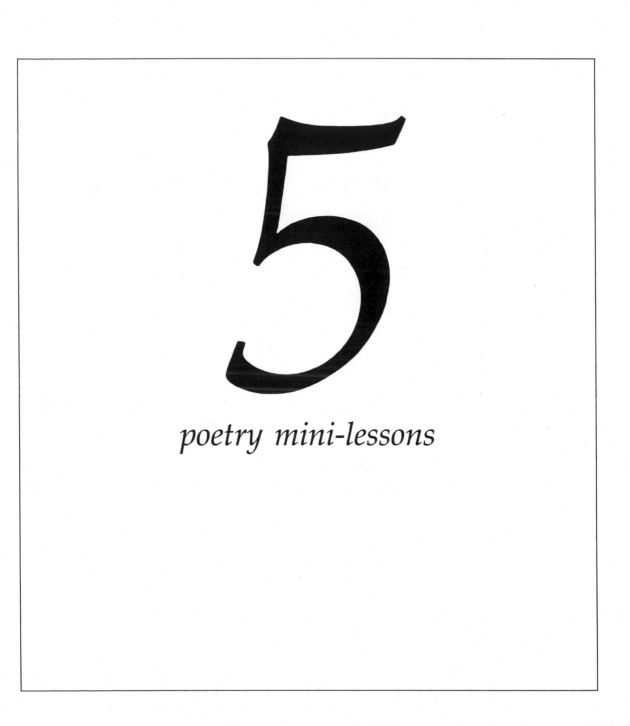

5

poetry mini-lessons

So much of writing poetry is fine-tuning and revision. Although there is always a certain tension in allowing a good burst of words to have life without undue tampering, I want to encourage children to keep trying poetry. I know that it may take many first drafts before a writer can begin to see the place of revision.

Revision comes from burning questions writers have about their intentions. I ask myself about the relationship between the text and my questions about my intentions in the poem. Of course, for a long time I may not even know my intentions. I simply put words down on paper. Or I may have a particular feeling that I want to resonate in my poem. During and after writing "Sunday at the Lake" I asked myself, "Does this poem sound angry? Do the details add up to what I want to say about people who mar a silent Sunday with their growling engines?"

Most of the mini-lessons in this chapter are not intended as lessons for an entire class. I don't expect that many children will be writing poetry at any one time. You will be able to apply these mini-lessons with two to four children at a time, in individual conferences, and occasionally while demonstrating with your own writing. You will recognize some familiar elements from the last chapter, where we worked to recognize children's potential as writers and to nudge children into new experiences. Those Actions will prepare you for the more formal mini-lesson.

As you demonstrate the writing of poetry and share the work of various poets with the class, children will group themselves into small clusters who choose to write poetry together. Some of the children will write poetry over weeks and months; others will come and go as their interest rises and falls. When this occurs it is quite natural for you to do mini-lessons with these clusters.

I call the group together several times a week to share our poetry with each other and to work at our texts in small mini-lessons. I use my work and the children's as the substance of the mini-lesson. The following are examples of the various aspects of poetry we consider in the mini-lessons as we work on our revisions and learn how to help each other write:

- Work with details.
- Work with sound and repetition.
- Work for more precise language.
- Review the origins of poetry.
- Help children to help each other.
- Review your collection of poems.

ACTION: WORK WITH DETAILS.

It is important to know where we usually leave out necessary or important details, for example, when we provide conclusions without the evidence to support them. A simple line like "They were sad" is a conclusion. What I need is evidence to show why people were sad.

> *After the flames died down,*
> *after the firemen*
> *rolled up their hoses,*
> *and the rumbles of their motors*
> *could no longer be heard*
> *on the other side of the river,*
> *the family began to poke*
> *randomly through the ashes.*

Now I have details that help the reader to feel sadness. Of course, with these details, there is no reason to write "They were sad."

At other times the details are simply not accurate. This deals more with word choice, which can be a separate mini-lesson.

Here is how I help a small group with a mini-lesson on details. It is basically a reading exercise. In fact, much of the work in these mini-lessons involves exercises in learning how to read our own poetry as well as the poetry of others. A spirit of discovery and play should set the tone of the mini-lessons. In this instance the children look for places in their work where they have made a general statement but have not provided the necessary details. I start with my own writing:

DON: I think I've found what I mean by not having enough evidence in something I've written. Listen to this:

> *I felt tense when the day*
> *first broke. I wondered*
> *where it was all headed.*

Okay, what do you need to know to help you understand my feeling?

CHILD: What made you tense?

DON: Right. I had so many meetings and I wasn't prepared.

CHILD: What did you mean "where it was all headed"?

DON: I wondered if people would think poorly of me, if I was sloppy or something. Let me try to show you how I'll be more detailed and specific using the information you asked me about.

> *My jaw was set,*
> *the muscles like light*
> *rubber bands almost made*
> *my teeth ache, meetings*
> *ahead made me wonder*
> *if this jury of readers*
> *would find me guilty*
> *of not preparing . . .*

That was kind of fast but what I did was take that word, "tense," and try to give you the details of tenseness, like the muscles in the jaw. Who else will try one?

CHILD: I think I have one here. In my poem here I said I was upset, but I don't think the details are here for you to know. I'll read the part.

The day was sad,
I felt so upset
I snapped at everyone,
It was like I wanted
to bite them.

DON: All right, who'd like to comment?

CHILD: I don't know why you are sad either . . .

CHILD: Well, I was sad because my friend, who I won't speak of here, said she was coming over and she didn't call or anything.

DON: Did you spend time waiting for the call? Like it was on your mind the whole evening?

CHILD: Sure.

DON: Okay, I hear details now that you can use. No call. The waiting. Expecting. And you were probably doing things while you were waiting and wondering. Maybe start with that information. Did I sense some kind of impatience while you were waiting?

CHILD: Yes, I was trying to do my homework and I couldn't think. She was coming over and we were going to do it together.

Later the child started the poem in the following way:

Waiting.
Waiting.
My foot tapping,
Pages turning in a book
I don't read.
No ring.
No hello.
No friend.

The short lines give the feeling of waiting and time going by slowly. The details of what made her sad and upset with her friend are now concrete. The audience understands more clearly what the writer means. Even more important, the writer understands more clearly how she felt as she relives the incident through her writing.

Although the focus of this mini-lesson is on details, it is virtually impossible to leave out other elements. The last writer, for example, was able to convey a mood in her short lines even though the mini-lesson didn't address mood. And how hard it is to teach mood.

I have a hunch that working with poets of any age involves providing opportunities for insight, helping them hear their own language, reading their favorite poets, and listening as they read their work aloud. The sound and sense of poetry hover inside the draft of a poem to emerge in the midst of trying to match language, line, and intention.

ACTION: **WORK WITH SOUND AND REPETITION.**

Sound and sense are an essential part of poetry. Sound, and its repetition, will be part of this mini-lesson. I recall this child who wrote a poem, "All We Know," after the *Challenger* disaster in 1986 (Newkirk and Atwell 1988, p. 125). She used a repeating line, "All we know. . . ."

ALL WE KNOW

All we know is that she lived in a small town called Concord,
That she had a family,
And that she was a social studies teacher.
All we know is that she had a dream to go to space,
That her dream almost came true,
That she was going to teach class while in space,
That she had a chance to explain to us about our outer world,
And that she took her son's teddybear to be the first in space.
All we know is that she and six others boarded the shuttle with
*   happiness and hope,*
That they had a good lift-off,
That millions of people were watching the launch,

And that they will never come back to tell us about their
*   discoveries.*
All we know is that seven moons will be named after them,
That the families agree that life must go on,
And that they will be missed.
All we hope is that they went in peace.

When the teacher asked the student how she hit upon those very apt words, the student replied, "They kept saying on TV on the day of the explosion, 'All we know at this time is blah, blah.' I kept hearing it, and I knew I wanted to use it."

Poets use repetition to evoke mood. I think of Shakespeare's line, "When in the sessions of sweet, silent thought." The repeated sibilant "s" is soothing, the very effect Shakespeare probably wanted us to feel in reading the line and the sonnet.

In this mini-lesson I want to show what I mean by everyday repetition of language. I'll brainstorm first, then use what I come up with in a poem to achieve a certain kind of effect. As I hope to show, poetry helps to make the ordinary unusual. Here's a short list of what I hear over and over in our household.

- *In the family:*
  "Has the dog been fed?"
  "What do you want for breakfast?"
  "What time will you be home?"
  "I'm tired of all this rain."
  "What's in the mail?"
  "Any calls?"
  "What time do you want to get up?"
  "What time is it?"
  "Do you have any wood in your bin?"
  "When do you plan to go to bed?"
- *On television:*
  "We play them one game at a time."
  "Their discussions were frank and open."
  "The market was marked by moderate trading."
  "It isn't over until it's over."

Now I'll use one of these in a five-minute exercise to show what
I mean by using a repeating line.

ANY CALLS?

Any calls?
Like mail I wonder if some
are first class,
a friendly exchange,
or some perfunctory mumble,
"What time is the meeting?"
"Can we have lunch
on Tuesday at The Bagelry?"

Any calls?
I dread the call from Detroit,
an unanswered letter written
last August; it is now November;
I am before the jury
of unanswered letters, guilty
in the first degree, willful
bypassed white missives
that want, want, want.

Any calls?
The good news call,
the grant of thousands,
a visit from the Millionaire;
Mr. Roberts called?
An ordinary name, behind
simplicity lies generosity,
a kindly face, open giving,
who has heard of our research
a surprise grant to innovate.

Any calls?
a call at 4:00 P.M. from Dad?
Dad doesn't call at 4:00 P.M.,

Dad doesn't call at 4:00 P.M.,
must be sick,
or in special need,
maybe I'd better call my brother
first; I see him sitting puzzled
taking the phone, reaching out.

Any calls?
from Timmy Consolo?
you're kidding,
we haven't seen each other
for years, and he called?
he didn't leave a number?
said he'd call back?
what a guy,
always good for a laugh,
seems like yesterday
when we last spoke.

Writing a first draft like this makes me feel a little uneasy, especially since it will appear in a published book. I hear your voices, "Anyone can do that. In fact, I can do better." Well, that's what I hope you're saying to yourselves.

I do like the feel of the repeating line. It helps readers to recall their own feelings about telephone calls and creates a bond between us. We've all asked the question. The repeat line also lets me relive deeper experiences of my own.

ACTION: WORK FOR MORE PRECISE LANGUAGE.

Keep in mind that at its heart, revision is connected with trying to match meaning with intention. I constantly explore in class, for the sake of writing and literacy in general, the big questions I ask of myself and the world I live in. If my questions about life and living are small ones and my quest for clarity is limited, then there is little need for revision. Revision is the result of itches that have to be scratched. My role as a teacher is to help students to itch at the point of their intentions.

When I work with words in a mini-lesson I start with my own writing. I want to show how I ask questions of the piece in relation to the larger intentions that spur me on. Of course, when I change a word it is because the context usually demands it. An abstract or nonspecific word requires questioning. When I look at my writing I look for pictures that are precise or imprecise. I ask myself:

- What adjectives could I remove by making the noun more precise?
- What adverbs could I remove by making the verb more precise?
- What pronouns should be changed to nouns?

Poets, like all writers, work for economy of language. Economy and clarity go hand in hand. The liberal use of words from vocabulary lists for the sake of display, erudition, and teacher approval ought to be discouraged. It is not the way of art.

Now, to show what I mean, I will demonstrate how I work with a first draft. I'll write a quick draft of a poem here because that is the best way to work with words in relation to what I am trying to say. The text I write here is for you, the teacher, and not necessarily what I would write for children:

VIEW

The sog of four days
of rain dims my eyes
to the shifting fog
that twirls and swirls
around the spruce tops
poking their gothic spires
through their own short heaven
in the valley. The verb

of fog is a hanging, pondering
elephant that dulls my eye
yet from my seat
has its own repertoire
of action, fast moving
delicate as lace blowing
before an open window.

I'll stop there. I'm writing in my study in Jackson, New Hampshire, which sits high in the White Mountains overlooking a winding valley. We've had four days of rain and fog. There are no mountain views and there seems to be a lack of the customary drama in this recent weather pattern. I know there is more to it, so I look out the window to show the verb of fog. The verb notion crept in, I suspect, because I was going to write still more about language in relation to this first draft.

Now that I've written the poem, I realize that I've got much more to do than adjust a few words here and there. Simply put, there are inaccuracies and many other elements to work on. I reread my poem with a critical eye. Reporting the experience more precisely will force me to revise my words:

The sog of four days
of rain dims my eyes
to the dancing *fog*
that twirls and swirls
around spruce tops
that poke their gothic spires
through their own gossamer
heaven in the valley.
The verb of fog* is a ponderous
elephant *that dulls my eyes.*

---

* The "verb of fog" was such an intriguing notion that months later I used it in another poem (see the Appendix).

In line three I changed "shifting" to "dancing." What I am trying to say here is that there is drama in the weather, even with four days of fog and rain. I get lulled into the notion that because of the fog, nothing is going on. But there is. It's like a slow dance. But "dancing," "whirling," and "twirling" are not the most accurate words for a slow dance. I can use "dance" if I can get the right word to go with it. Actually, it's a courtly minuet. I'll try that.

> *The sog of four days*
> *of rain dims my eyes*
> *to the* courtly *fog*
> *that twirls and swirls*
> a minuet *around spruce*
> *tops, gothic spires*
> brashly declaring election
> to their low heaven
> *in the valley.*

I'm beginning to get the feel I want in the text with the addition of "courtly" and "minuet." I want to give a dignified feeling to the way the fog moves. The fog swirls around the tips of the spruce trees, which stand above the layers of fog. In the original draft I said the spruce trees "poked" their way through the fog, but that isn't the feeling I want. There is something bold rather than pastoral in the way the treetops stand above the fog. It is almost as if the trees have some kind of superior level of being in their declaration of election to their kind of heaven.

But I'm still uneasy. In the last draft there are too many words, especially in the "brashly declaring," and the text isn't as active and immediate as I want it to be. I'll go to work to change both in this new draft:

> Four days of rain and sog
> dim my eyes to the courtly fog
> *that twirls and swirls a minuet*

around spruce tops, gothic spires
that declare election
to their low heaven.

I've kept the text active by making the verbs present tense. I want to feel—and I want the reader to feel—the immediacy of my observations. Present tense is my favorite for writing poetry. It makes for more active poems.

THE MINI-LESSON: I revise because there is a mismatch between my intention
A REFLECTION   and the words on the page. My language does not match the questions I want to address in the text. As I go to work on the text, I maintain a spirit of exploration and play. I do not berate myself because I did poorly on my first try, I merely enter into a new phase of play. I find that children often don't want to revise because they think it means that their first draft was somehow wrong. My mini-lesson begins with an exploration of intentions.

The size of the group for this kind of mini-lesson should be small—no more than five children. We go around the group describing our intentions in the poems we have just written. "This is what I set out to do." "This is why I wrote this poem." "This is what I wanted to learn." "This is what I wanted to show." These are some of the many ways in which we express our intentions. I usually begin a share session with this kind of discussion of intention. Of course, sometimes I don't know why I am writing a poem. My intentions are confused, and I write to find out what they are. I may not even know until I have completed the poem, maybe not until months or years later. "Oh, *that's* what I was trying to do." Still, I keep searching and exploring, trying to keep in touch with my intentions.

Next, we explore ways to match our intentions with our language. I find that verbs are a good place to begin to toy with our drafts. Verbs often require the most attention. (Note how much attention I had to give to verbs in my last piece.) I'll put the verbs in roman.

> *Four days of rain and sog*
> dim *my eyes to the courtly fog*
> *that* twirls *and* swirls *a minuet*
> *around spruce tops, gothic spires*
> *that* declare *election*
> *to their low heaven.*

Many of my changes were dictated by "dim" and "declare" and by the tone set by "twirls" and "swirls."

Ask the children to underline the action words in their poems. Discuss how well these words express their intentions in writing the poem. Try to elicit more precise words for those they have underlined. Again, the tone should be one of experimentation and play. "If you change that word, what have you got? Do you find that interesting?"

For some children, changing verbs may lead to changes in adverbs or in the nouns that relate to the verbs. During the mini-lesson I point out examples of strong verbs. For very young children who do not know the meaning of *verb*, I say, "Oh, that is a strong verb; I can see just what the horse is doing. He *prances*. Does that mean he goes just like this [*I stand and demonstrate*] when he is in place?" I then act out the verb or ask the child to do it.

DON: Who would like to share a poem in which you sense some parts don't work as you intended? First tell what you had in mind, then read a part that you'd like to work with.

JAN: Well, I wanted to show how really beautiful this place was that we went swimming on a very hot day. It was special, only it doesn't sound special at all. I don't even know why I'm sharing this.

DON: Sounds like you have nothing to lose by sharing it.

JAN: Oh yes I do. I don't want anyone to laugh.

DON: I'm sorry. I guess I said that too quickly. We'll really try to help. If you want to back out at any point just say, "That's it!" Okay?

JAN: Okay. I already told you what I wanted and that it doesn't work. Here's what I've got so far:

> *The water spilled down*
> *through rocks, over boulders,*
> *then ran down to the dam below.*

DON: Okay, Jan, you feel something is missing. Let's forget what's here. Say what you think is missing.

JAN: Oh, the water was so cold it made your teeth ache. But there was shade. Big trees were overhead and if you looked down they made patterns on the water. And then there was the sound of it. It gurgled. That's a dumb word. Everybody says brooks gurgle. But I don't have another one so I didn't write anything.

DON: Let's stop there. You've seen so much, Jan. I've written some things here from your words:

> *cold water—teeth ache.*
> *trees overhead*
> *patterns on the water*
> *(gurgled—sound of the water)*

I'd like to hear the group's reaction to what you've noticed.

CHILD: You could use what you saw in the trees. Sounded kind of filmy the way the light came through.

CHILD: How did the water come down? Could you tell me how it did that?

JAN: It came down like it was coming down steps, first one level, then another. It had this steady coming down, the sound never stopped. But I don't know the right sound yet.

CHILD: Well, could you think of something else that makes that same sound?

JAN: Hmmm, it was a deep sound. I've got to think about that.

DON: We've explored quite a bit here. Jan, you started with what you thought was missing. We've mentioned what that was, so just try writing that part. As far as the sound is concerned, we suggested that you think of something else that sounded that way; that will take you into metaphor. Put it aside for a while. Perhaps something will come to you.

I have brought the children into the mini-lesson to get experience in learning what helps others as well as what helps themselves. I don't want too many suggestions or details to muddy the water. Thus, I end with Jan exploring some of the elements she thought were missing from her poem. The sound of the water is a challenge. I want her to know that a metaphor may come to her sometime. I also want the other children to recognize that putting a piece aside can sometimes be a good strategy.

DELETION   When children learn that some words or lines in their poems are more important than others, deletion is a natural by-product. But until we can establish together just how important something in a child's poem is, and until children see that something else may have more value, deletion is difficult for them. A separate mini-lesson on deletion is thus not feasible, but deletion does come up during other mini-lessons. When children decide to delete, we discuss how they were able to make that decision.

ACTION: REVIEW THE ORIGINS OF POETRY.

This action is probably not one you will do consciously. It is more likely that you will occasionally check to see if children are aware of how their poems originate. Here are some ways to encourage children to think about how poems develop:

- Share your intentions (as in the mini-lesson on working with revision).
- Periodically discuss the inspiration behind a poem when the poetry group meets—an image, an experience, a feeling.
- When you compose, whether with your small group or with the entire class, tell where your own poems come from, as well as why you chose some of your images and metaphors.
- When you and the children read the poems of professional poets, speculate on their origin. Also, be sure to share a wide range of poems on all sorts of subjects.

ACTION: HELP CHILDREN TO HELP EACH OTHER.

One of the objectives of our poetry group meetings is to demonstrate practices group members can apply on their own when they help each other. I do some of the following to see if we are achieving this objective:

- Review what helps most in the group. How can we apply it in working with each other? Have the children show how they would do this in their own small group meeting.
- Have children regularly read their poems aloud in the group. Have them listen for:
  - Words that strike them.
  - Sounds that strike them.
  - How the poem (overall) affected them.
  - Where possible, ask writers to share their intention before reading. Have writers say what help they want before they read a poem.
- Be sure to share your own poems as part of the group session. Find out for yourself what is helpful.

ACTION:　REVIEW YOUR COLLECTION OF POEMS.

Every poem has its own history. Part of having a sense of that history is looking at our work from many points of view. We all have different thoughts and feelings about our work. This mini-lesson is intended to help us look at a collection of our own work. Before I begin this exercise I ask the children to choose four to six of their poems, reread them, and place them on the desk or table in front of them. I suggest a maximum of eight poems and a minimum of four for this exercise to be helpful. The children will need a pencil to participate, and since they will be making short notes on each of the poems, some of the children may want to attach small pieces of paper to each poem. I've found that some children do not like to write again on something they consider "final copy."

TEACHER: Choose your poems now, reread them, and place them on the table in front of you. Okay, I'd like you to choose two that you like more than the others. You may not know why you like them, you just do. Write LIKE at the top of those with your pencil.

[*Be sure to allow time for the children to reread, since some of these discovery tasks will require more time. Observe them while they are doing this. You can sense in your own search the level of difficulty and the time required. If the children finish too soon and you are still working, it may mean they do not understand the task.*]

Choose one poem that was hard to write. Write HARD at the top.

Choose one poem that was fun and easy to write. Write FUN/EASY at the top.

Look over your poems and find a place where the words make a good picture. Underline that place and then write PICTURE at the top.

Find a place where you like the *sounds* in the line. You

may need to read some of your lines aloud to see if you like them. After you find the place, underline it, then write SOUNDS at the top.

Find a poem you wrote when you had very strong feelings. Write FEELINGS at the top.

Find a poem in which you felt you wrote best what you intended to write. That is, when you finished, you felt you had done exactly what you intended. This will take a little time to think through for each one. When you find that poem, write INTENDED at the top.

Find a poem in which you felt you learned the most about writing poetry. Write LEARN at the top.

Find a poem you would like to return to to work on again some day. You won't work on it today, but you'll return to it again in the future. Write RETURN at the top.

Find the poem that you've enjoyed sharing the most with the group and with others. When you find that poem write SHARE at the top.

Find the poem on which you've received the best help from others. Write HELP at the top.

You will find many other ways for children to look at their work. In time, the children will suggest traits of their own to mark at the top of their poems.

Many of the poems will have many different words on them, and some of the traits may seem contradictory. Discuss the range of observations and traits the children have listed on their pieces. Don't forget to share your observations about your own.

FINAL REFLECTION   Poetry is only one genre children will work with at any one time in the classroom. Others will be writing personal narratives, fiction, or essays. Sometimes I demonstrate poetry writing with the entire class in order to introduce the genre to the children. Most of the time, however, I conduct poetry sessions with a small group (from three to seven children) who happen to be writing poetry at that time. One to two group sessions weekly, of about fifteen minutes' duration, is about as much as I have time to handle. The makeup of the group is constantly shifting. Some children may stay with a group for as long as two months, while others may only stay for two weeks. This means that group membership is constantly changing as some children leave and others start writing poetry for the first time.

The spirit of the poetry group should be one of enjoyment, exploration, and experimentation. Poetry is particularly well-suited to mini-lessons because most poems are fairly short. Using our poems, the children and I explore new ways of working with words and appreciating poetry. We also share our own poetry and the work of our favorite poets.

6

three teachers

Bill Keagle teaches fifth grade in a metropolitan suburb. Bill was a science major in college. He came to teaching after a short career in business. "Deep down," Bill says, "I always knew I wanted to be a teacher. I've finally come home. I like kids, science, and that sense of discovering things. I've been working with writing and reading for two years. Took a writing course in a summer program and I've just begun to see what writing and reading can mean for my kids when they get to choose their topics and genre. I teach poetry in an eight-day concentration, and I'm just beginning to use it in my science and social studies. I'm not real comfortable with it but I'm pleased with how I'm growing. Science majors, you know, aren't too comfortable with this English stuff."

Beryl Bednark teaches second grade in a small city. "I'm not sure if writing or even poetry is for my kids but I'm willing to give it a go. It is in our curriculum guide. I notice that our new literature-based reading program has an assortment of good poems and I'll use those during my poetry concentration." Beryl hasn't had much preparation for working with either writing or poetry. "My own experiences with poetry," cautions Beryl, "make me feel like I do when I'm holding a newborn baby . . . something might break if I do more than just hold it. I don't want to be the teacher who turns the kids off of poetry."

Sheila Tetelson is a sixth-grade teacher in a country school. Sheila loves poetry and has read and written it for as long as she can remember. When she was growing up, her family read poems aloud, often reciting them from memory. Sheila freely admits that she could teach poetry "all day long and every day of the school year." "My battle," she says, "is to keep my poetry reflex in check and let the children read and write other things."

I have chosen these three teachers to show how each attempts to surround children with poetry—in a unique way. All three are trying to grow in the teaching of poetry as well as in the writing and reading of poetry itself. I present them here to

89

illustrate several different starting points for teachers who wish to bring poetry into their professional repertoire, and to show how poetry can be an integral part of the teaching day.

BILL KEAGLE "I've just begun to make the connection between poetry and science," says Bill Keagle. "When my kids take field notes on their science work I push them for details. They don't see the world all that clearly, and that makes them poor scientists. Well, I've gotten hold of some good stuff poets write about the outdoors and I can see now how the two connect, poetry and good science. Both require detail. For some of my slower kids, I have them read basic illustrated books by Ruth Heller. I can deal with both the information and details of the subject in that way."

Bill began to change both the course of his teaching and his work with reading and writing through an intensive summer course. He found that he had things to say and that others reacted to his "crusty" (as he put it) way of blurting things out in his texts. People laughed but they also took his notions seriously. He is frank to say that his students write more non-fiction than fiction—more field notes and science and social studies reports—simply because what he reads aloud is more in the nonfiction genre.

"I provide roughly an hour for my students to read and write. First thing in the morning. They have a choice as to what they'll write and read about. I conduct mini-lessons on the various skills. I suppose I should provide more time but I figure the reading and writing they do in social studies and science counts for something. They have a choice about what they'll read and write there as well, though there are some things they absolutely must read and write."

This year Bill has decided to concentrate for various periods on different genres. Poetry is one of his concentrations. Others are fiction, personal narrative, and argument (the beginnings of exposition). "I want the children at least to be exposed to various ways of writing and reading. I believe in choice but I think it ought to be more informed by actual practice in the genres so that when something comes up in class that they ought to experiment with—like a good argument for changing the lunch room or something in this class—they can do it." As Bill implies in his statement, he likes to pick up on instances in class or individual life when writing and reading can be used in a more timely and relevant fashion.

Bill used eight days at the end of September to introduce his class to poetry (see Figure 6–1). In the reading/writing block he allotted sixty minutes to working with poetry. First, he went to the library to get a wide range of poetry, both to read aloud and to allow his children to select their own reading. Bill's taste in poetry leaned toward the humorous and anything connected with the outdoors. Although Ruth Heller's poetry was more for younger students, Bill liked the scientific precision of her poems along with the illustrations.

Robert Frost surprised him. He remembered hating his poems in junior high school (*hate* was the actual word he used), but now he was struck by Frost's observations and their linkage to real-life questions. Bill was an outdoorsman and was surprised to find that Frost was too. "The Pasture Spring," "A Tuft of Flowers," and "The Road Not Taken" were some of his favorite Frost poems.

Bill started each class session with a poetry reading. He prepared at home, reading the poems aloud several times. By the end of the third day, he asked children to read some of their own favorite poems or poets aloud to the class, as well as some of the pieces they were writing. As a condition for reading aloud, he asked that they first practice reading to a partner or use the tape recorder to listen to themselves reading. When they thought they were ready, they could share with the class.

This year Bill tried two new poetry practices: composing a poem with the class and choral speaking. He was more confident about writing the poem than about the choral speaking.

WEEK ONE	Monday	Tuesday	Wednesday	Thursday	Friday
Teacher does	Propose/select books Read poetry aloud	Read poetry aloud Write a list poem Respond to children's list poems Ⓝ	Show how he fleshes out list poems Ⓝ	Introduce poetry starters Read poetry aloud Poetry conferences Small group share	Introduce poetry starters Read poetry aloud Poetry conferences
Children do	Read from poetry books	Listen to reading Try list poems Read from books	Practice partners Share poetry Read aloud books, own poetry Reading letter	Read/write poetry Group share	Read/write poetry Group share

WEEK TWO	Monday	Tuesday	Wednesday	Thursday	Friday
Teacher does	Start choral speaking Ⓝ Compose poem in class Conference	Choral speak Conferences	Read poems from science aloud Compose poems in class—science		
Children do	Learn poems from choral speaking Group share Read/write poetry	3 children read poem aloud Group share Read/write poetry	3 children read poetry aloud Ⓝ Group share Read/write poetry Letter on reading		

FIGURE 6–1 BILL KEAGLE'S EIGHT-DAY PLAN—SUSTAINED (60 MINUTES EACH DAY)

Continue with:
- Occasional poetry group
- Poetry in science
- Writing to class occasionally
- Choral speaking
- Publishing class collection of poetry in science together

On own:

Ⓝ = New skill this year

After reading several poems aloud to the class, he decided to introduce composing a poem. He debated whether to write "cold turkey" in class with no preparation or to practice at home. He decided to practice at home.

Several days before, when they were on a field trip, the class had discovered a Golden Orb spider in the middle of a web strung between a cluster of milkweed pods. He decided to try poetry by first doing a list or column poem on the spider:

> *web*
> *dew drops*
> *shimmer*
> *silver*
> *black*
> *spider*
> *gold band*
> *menacing*
> *dangerous?*
> *waiting*
> *watchful*
> *piece of moth*
> *look out*

He put the words on an overhead projector and asked the class if there were other words that came to mind. The words could be seeing words or feeling words, he told them. He asked the class to make a list of other things they saw on the field trip. He posted the list; then children could choose an item from the list and try a list poem of their own, showing details and telling about their feelings.

On the second day Bill showed the class how he took his list and began to flesh out his poem:

> *Yellow on black,*
> *shimmering on a web,*
> *a death dance*

to any moth or insect,
the Golden Orb spider
waits, watchful
as an evil queen.

He asked the children to try a poem from their list as he just demonstrated. Some wished to abandon their first list and try a new one; others continued. A few children didn't write at all. Bill conferred with them in small clusters of five. "I'm a systematic person; maybe it's my science background, but I sort of like everyone to be together the first three or four days."

Bill circulated through the class, responding to the poems the children composed from their lists. He received their work, commenting on the details and the feelings but also asking questions: "I'd like to see a little more detail." "Well, how do you feel about that?"

For the last two days in the week Bill introduced several starter choices:

• On the playground I saw . . .
• I am the person who . . .

If children were comfortable writing list poems, they could start there. Bill intended that the first week be devoted to demonstrations and starters and the second week to a choice of poem topic or process. He usually wrote with the children.

Children also read from books of poetry. Bill had ten library books, and some children brought poetry books from home to augment the collection. Bill told them, "There are twice as many of you as there are books; that means you'll need to share your books as much as you can." He asked children to make lists of the poems and authors they liked as well as particular lines in poems. Every three days they would write a letter to him about their reading and include some of the information he asked them to keep, and he wrote letters back to each child, commenting on what they had seen in the poetry and sharing some of his own reactions.

The most difficult challenge Bill Keagle undertook with the children was his move into choral speaking in the second week. He had no trouble learning the poem, but conducting a class was another story. He felt like an impostor standing in front of the class conducting them through the rhythm and saying the poem with them. "I just wave my arms and hope I'm right. At least we start together with the first line," he says, "but the children seem to learn and enjoy, so I guess I'll continue. I'm not sure if I'll ever get used to it."

BERYL BEDNARK   Beryl Bednark has taught for nine years, but she is teaching poetry for the first time. She is apprehensive. She provides for three sessions of writing each week, a considerable increase over last year, when the children didn't write at all.

A major contributor to Beryl's change of direction was her attendance at a regional workshop the previous year in which she learned about writing as a means of expression for city children. The samples of written work by children from multi-ethnic backgrounds intrigued her. "I'm sort of at a threshold personally and professionally (I'm thirty years old next fall, you know) and I want a change of direction. It's a little terrifying, but fortunately I won't have to do it alone." Beryl's school colleague and friend, Margaret Zolnick, was the person who invited her to attend the original writing workshop and volunteered to help her get started with writing. Coincidentally, Margaret taught poetry along with writing. Beryl followed Margaret's lead.

Beryl started to work with poetry in the third week of September. "I had to get the children settled in before I tried anything like poetry," she reasoned. She observed Margaret reading and sharing poetry with her own third-grade class. "I know I won't sound like Margaret when I read," she said, "but I'll try."

Beryl chose three of the poems Margaret used when she started reading aloud to her own children. By the time Beryl finished practicing her poems, she was surprised to find herself enjoying them. "It just feels good, that's all," she said. (Beryl's five-day plan is shown in Figure 6–2.)

Margaret loaned her some extra poetry books for her "poetry week." Beryl also used all nine poems in their literature-based reading book. Although the poems were spaced throughout the book, Beryl chose to use them all at once to give the children a "jump start" into poetry. Beryl chose Shel Silverstein's (1964) poems "Sister for Sale" and "Cynthia Sylvia Semantha Stout . . . wouldn't take the garbage out" for their humor. She was comfortable with humor.

The most difficult step for Beryl was helping children to write poetry of their own. "I've never written any. How on earth am I going to help them get started? Besides, so many of them have trouble with their reading. They're only second graders, you know," she complained to Margaret.

Margaret helped her to realize that poetry is a matter of seeing well and choosing details to evoke the feelings that go with the seeing. Looking and describing carefully sometimes result in poems with sound repetition. One afternoon after school, Margaret showed Beryl how to explore a list poem by composing one quickly with her. "Here's a geranium plant with several blossoms on it. We'll try a list poem from it. We'll say details— the words or feelings that are triggered by the plant. And we'll alternate when we do it. I'll go first, then you."

MARGARET: odor
BERYL: greenhouse
MARGARET: red flashing
BERYL: memories
MARGARET: branching
BERYL: watering
MARGARET: stiff, strong

FIGURE 6–2   BERYL BEDNARK'S FIVE-DAY PLAN (50 MINUTES EACH DAY)

	Monday	Tuesday	Wednesday	Thursday	Friday
Teacher does	Read poetry aloud Ⓝ	Read poem aloud Tries list poem Ⓝ	Read poem aloud Responds to children's poetry Ⓝ	Read poem aloud Tries another list poem Responds to children's poetry	
Children do	Read poetry from reader	Children try list poem with teacher Read poetry Share some lists for those who volunteer Ⓝ	Read poetry Share reading of some favorite poems	Try list poem again Children share jointly with Ms. Zolnick's class	Children illustrate their list poems

Ⓝ = New skill this year

<u>After school:</u>
Meets again with Margaret to see how to expand on list poem

<u>Continue with:</u>
• Publishing collection of poems
• Sharing oral reading of poems
• Writing poetry (a few children)

BERYL: caring
MARGARET: windowsill
BERYL: royal

Beryl was surprised at the ease with which the words came and the sense of clarity of what to do with her children. "I can see where you could take that and continue on with a poem. I think I'll do the same with the class tomorrow. I'll choose something from the room, and we'll try a list poem with it on experience chart paper. I'll alternate with them the way you did with me." Beryl borrowed a rabbit from the kindergarten class to use for the poem. And it worked. Children catalogued the specific attributes of the rabbit, how it hopped and ate as well as their reaction to it, in list fashion on the paper. Later they chose their own objects and used invented spelling to write their own lists.

Most of Beryl's poetry time that week was spent reading poems aloud, making list poems, and using the poems from the readers. The children also shared their list poems, their impressions, and how they were writing at the end of their reading/writing time in poetry. Beryl followed some of Margaret's sharing time procedures:

- Child reads the poem.
- The class first tells
  - what pictures they see in the words.
  - what struck them.
  - what they feel (related as much as possible to the details).
- The class asks questions on what they'd like to know more about.

The children use this process with their own poetry and with the poetry they hear or read in their books.

One caution: Although Beryl is using a rather specific sharing sequence, it is important to vary the sharing as much as possible. It is too easy to fall into a pro forma response pattern, which can take the place of a more sensitive response.

SHEILA TETELSON   Sheila Tetelson spent two straight weeks on poetry with her sixth-grade class and maintained small poetry response groups from September through June. (Her two-week plan is shown in Figure 6–3.) Sheila is comfortable with all aspects of poetry. Last year she experimented with using poetry throughout the curriculum and also tried to build a collection of poetry that served the broader aspects of the curriculum.

"I start the first day of school in September with choral speaking," reports Sheila. "I do that for several reasons. First, it is so easy to help children learn poetry that way. Within two days they'll learn the best part of three poems by heart. Second, they'll find out how much fun poetry is if they pick it up through the ear first. Third, if they know the poems, like songs, they'll carry the sound and rhythm with them no matter where they are. Fourth, when our entire class knows something together like that we become a community very quickly; we have that feeling of "look what we can do."

In addition to the fifteen minutes Shelia spent on choral speaking each day for the first week, she also introduced three to four books of poetry by reading several poems aloud from each book daily. During her twelve-year teaching career Sheila has built up a collection of more than thirty-five books of poetry, which she makes available to the children. "I'd like you all to read through several of these poetry books over the next two weeks and find some poems you like. When you find them, set up a meeting with a partner and share what you are discovering. At the end of our morning session tomorrow I'll ask for a few volunteers to share what they've found; you might even like the poem enough to read it aloud. If you do decide to share it, please practice reading it ahead of time."

Sheila has been writing poetry herself for the last three years. Some she shares with the children; some she even writes about

FIGURE 6–3 SHEILA TETELSON'S TWO-WEEK PLAN (80 MINUTES EACH DAY)

WEEK ONE	Monday	Tuesday	Wednesday	Thursday	Friday

Teacher does	Choral speak
	List poem write
	Poetry
	  conference
	Reading poetry
	  aloud
		Choral speak
		Demo expand
		  list poem
		Intro to three
		  poets
			Choral speak
			Poetry
			  conferences
				Intro to first
				  lines
				Poetry
				  conferences
					Choral speak
					Writes poem
					  about class
					  event
					Poetry
					  conferences

Children do	Choral speak
	List poem write
	Share poetry
	  progress
		Choral speak
		Expand list
		  poem
		Children read
		  poems
			Choral speak
			Write and
			  refine list
			  poems
			Share poems
			  (own and
			  others)
				Try first line
				  poem actions
				Share (own and
				  others)
					Choral speak
					Read and write
					  poems
					Share own
					  poetry and
					  others

WEEK TWO	Monday	Tuesday	Wednesday	Thursday	Friday

Teacher does	Demo
	Find poems
	Intro new poet
	Mini-lesson
		Find poems
		  demo
		Choral speak
		Intro new poet
		Mini-lesson
			Find poems
			  demo, out
			  of doors
			  (combine
			  with science)
			Mini-lesson
				Share lyrics,
				  contemporary
				  music
				Conference—
				  small group
				  that will
				  continue to
				  write poetry
					First poetry
					  publication
					Conference—
					  small group
					  poetry

Children do	Read and write
	  poetry
	New poem
	Experiment
	  with list lines
	Participate in
	  mini-lesson
		Read and write
		  poetry
		Children share
		  "found"
		  poems
		Participate in
		  mini-lesson
			Go outside,
			  observe, take
			  notes
			Share reading
			  and writing
			Mini-lesson
				Read and write
				  poetry—
				  student
				  choice
				Share reading
				  and writing
				Mini-lesson
					Read and write
					  poetry—
					  student
					  choice
					Share reading
					  and writing

Maintain poetry
● Choral speaking
● Reading poems aloud
● Small group meetings for reading and writing
● Composing poetry herself
● Looking for poetry sources
● Poetry mini-lessons

specific events that arise in class. She wants the children to see how poetry can reflect the very things that happen from day to day. On one particular restless morning in February, when the barometer was dropping and the weather forecast was heavy snow, she composed a quick, first-draft poem on chart paper while the children were out at recess:

A HINT OF SNOW

The first flimsy snowflakes
come spiraling down
at about 10:15,
and with them a rising
chorus of "there they are;
early dismissal,
forts to build,"
a crescendo
of voices and excitement
like the promise
of Christmas morning;
David Walker dreams
of a ski trip and Alison
Weeks thinks of snow
angels, and I hear
the muffled silence
of snow when I turn
in bed on a no-school day.

Sheila clamped the poem up on the easel and asked the children to read it aloud together. She wanted them to feel the poem for themselves in the reading. Then she asked, "All right, What strikes you? What pictures do you see? What do you want to know more about?"

Sheila introduces the writing of poetry during the first week of school through the same simple list poems used by Bill and Beryl. She'll demonstrate list poems for two days and first line starters another day, and end by looking for poems in published prose or in the children's prose. Her idea is to surround the children with poetry by reading it aloud, by involving them in choral speaking, by introducing various ways to start poems, and by looking for the sources of poems where poems arise in their lives.

The first week consisted of an all-class immersion in poetry and a little work in small groups. At the end of poetry time the children shared their experiences with the process and read their favorite poems and some of their own poetry aloud.

But some children found it difficult to start writing poetry. "Letting go" to write words quickly was particularly hard for some of the perfectionists. Another group, already in early adolescence, were particularly fearful of what other students might say. "Oh, this is dumb. Ratty!" Sheila noted some covering their papers. Another group had the "sillies." Thoroughly self-conscious, they giggled and cast sidelong glances at each other. Sheila is not surprised at some of this behavior and expects a certain amount of uneasiness from some of the children. Unless it disturbs the class, she ignores it. She knows that her own writing with the class and the choral speaking dispels the self-consciousness rather quickly.

A good number of her sixth graders are usually interested in contemporary music and can list the top twenty tunes with accuracy. Sheila looks for some of the best of these and reads the lyrics on the inside folders of the CDs aloud. Sometimes she copies them and puts them on an acetate for the overhead projector. Children critique the lines, saying which ones strike them—or don't. It isn't long before the children ask to share the lyrics of some of their own favorite songs.

During the second week some of the children were ready to work on some of the poems they had started the first week. Sheila continued to involve the children in short mini-lessons to help them discover new entry points to poetry. Her demonstrations were short, and the children wrote immediately afterward. In the second week (see Figure 6–3) she introduced "found" poems (see Chapter 7)—finding poems outdoors, or in contemporary music. The children worked on poems just long enough to give them a "taste," about ten minutes. At the end of the mini-lesson some children returned to reading poetry or writing poems already under way.

Sheila's work with the children outdoors was part of her attempt to open up poetry across the curriculum. Science was not her area of expertise. She was a "seer," but not in the scientific sense. She read some of Ruth Heller's work to begin to discover opportunities for poetry and to acquaint herself with science. She also enlisted the help of another faculty member who was better versed in science and did a walk-through of the woods across the street from the school to begin to understand observation more clearly. Later in the year Sheila also tried the "motion" study as a prelude to writing poetry, and the "number" study in order to expand poetry into the curriculum (see Chapter 9).

On the last day of the second week Sheila announced that a small group of six children would continue writing poetry beyond the intensive two-week introduction. The group would commit itself to two weeks of writing poetry and meet with her twice weekly. At the end of two weeks those who wished to continue would stay and those who wished to leave would be replaced by other children who wished to join. Sheila met with the groups all year long and thus any children who wished to focus on poetry could do so. The maximum length of time children stayed in the group was four weeks, although they could continue to write poetry on their own if they wished.

At the end of two weeks, Sheila continued poetry, but on a more informal basis. Figure 6–3 indicates that she continued choral speaking. She actually did this two to three times a week, teaching new poems and practicing those the children already knew. The three to four minutes while waiting in line, preparing for lunch, or walking to music, art, or gym were ideal times to tuck in some choral speaking.

Throughout the year Sheila:

- Read poems aloud and introduced new poets.
- Composed poetry herself.
- Looked for poetry sources across the curriculum.
- Met with the small poetry group twice weekly.
- Conferred with children who wrote poetry during morning conferences.

THREE TEACHERS: WHAT'S NEW?

All three of these teachers work with poetry. Of the three, Beryl Bednark is the most ambitious since she is attempting to add more new elements to her teaching repertoire than Sheila or Bill. As Figure 6–4 shows, everything in the curriculum is new to her. She has only been working with writing itself for the last year. Fortunately, her colleague Margaret Zolnick can observe and confer with her about her teaching. The addition of poetry to her repertoire is a substantial step for her. Next year she will probably venture into publishing children's poetry and using poetry across the curriculum and throughout the day.

Bill Keagle's greatest learning step, even more than writing poetry with the children, was to try choral speaking with them. Fortunately, Bill is used to leaping into new things, and the choral speaking was not nearly as difficult as he had anticipated. As he said, "The image of me directing them like a choir director just didn't fit with the picture I have of myself as a teacher. But I just let go and hacked at it and it worked. You don't have to be smooth in conducting as much as you really need to know that poem and enjoy it." Next year he will do more publishing of children's poetry. He also wants to maintain a poetry group throughout the year and views this as his next great challenge.

Sheila Tetelson's greatest new step this year was using poetry

FIGURE 6–4   USE OF POETRY CURRICULUM

	Bill Keagle	Beryl Bednark	Sheila Tetelson
1. Teacher reads poetry aloud	X	Ⓝ X	X
2. Children read poetry from books	X	Ⓝ X	X
3. Writes poetry	Ⓝ X	Ⓝ X	X
4. Responds to children's poetry	X	Ⓝ X	X
5. Uses choral speaking	Ⓝ X	——	X
6. Uses poetry across the curriculum	X	Y	Ⓝ X
7. Length of introduction to poetry	8 days	5 days	10 days
8. Children share poetry (small group, whole class)	Ⓝ X	Ⓝ X	X
9. Maintains a small poetry group throughout the year	Y	——	Ⓝ X
10. Children read poetry aloud to class	Ⓝ X	Ⓝ X	X
11. Publishes children's poetry	Y	Y	X
12. Length of reading/writing poetry period	60 min.	50 min.	80 min.

Ⓝ = new to teacher
X = uses
Y = may try next year

in science. "The hard part," she said, "was in integrating something I knew a lot about with something I knew a little about." Maintaining a small group of children who continued to write poetry throughout the year was not difficult, although it was not easy for her to keep track of those who wanted to be part of the group. "Organization has always been a hard one for me," she reflected. Next year Sheila would like to broaden her demonstration and concentrate on several other genres, especially argument and fiction. "My specialty has always been poetry, and I have a hunch that the children's poetry would be stronger if they tried different kinds of writing."

FINAL REFLECTION All three teachers have immersed themselves and their students in poetry, but in their own ways. Two of the teachers, Bill Keagle and Beryl Bednark, feel somewhat uncomfortable with poetry, yet they were pleasantly surprised that by reading and writing poetry themselves they discovered a new personal enjoyment along with the children.

All three teachers surround themselves with poetry before they engage the children. They practice reading poetry aloud, they explore list or column poems at home, they memorize a few poems, and they read over poetry books from the library. They look for poems that please them, knowing that if they enjoy the poems, the children also will.

The teachers concentrate on poetry and surround children with poetry to let them experience it firsthand. All three read poetry aloud daily because poetry, more than other kinds of writing, needs to be read aloud. At the same time, although each teacher's plans reflect an individual approach to teaching, they all seek to involve children in reading and writing poetry.

Teachers stretch themselves as learners so that children can do the same. More important than the quality and range of the experiences with poetry children have in these three classrooms is the degree to which these teachers demonstrate their own learning as literate persons.

7

*continue to grow
with poetry*

Poetry can be a lifelong pursuit. When you tried the Actions in Chapter 3, I hope you began to feel the possibility that poetry could take hold in other corners of your life. Think about the power of poetry when occasions for writing and thinking arise. You will see and listen to the world differently. It will be magnified a hundredfold. You will hear poems in everyday speech, even in the ceiling fan that makes a slight sound with each revolution.

This chapter helps you to continue to incorporate poetry in your life and in the lives of the children you teach. I want children to make connections between poetry and the living world around them. Although children may be at home with poetry in the classroom, and poems are triggered by the many things that go on there, the outdoors also provides many opportunities for poetry. Just as the children take poetry with them in the many poems they know through choral speaking (Chapter 8), they also find poems in the everyday. Whether your classroom is in an urban, a rural, or a suburban setting, there is poetry in each season, in new leaves, in the passing of automobiles at a busy intersection.

As I write, I am at my home in the mountains in Jackson, New Hampshire. In a few minutes I'll go outdoors to "find" some poems. I'll take a pad of paper with me to see what might trigger a poem. Poems come to me as I wonder, "Oh, what is that?" "How come this is the case?" "That's a strange-looking thing. How come?" As Lewis Thomas writes in *Late Night Thoughts on Listening to Mahler's Ninth Symphony*, "Wonder is something to wonder about." If we look into the etymological background of the word *wonder*, we find "humor" at its root. We see something wonderful and a smile automatically comes to our lips. There is the "aha!" of beauty. I'm going outdoors now to make a list; I'll write when I return.

After fifteen minutes I'm back with a list. I'll probe each item with a few lines to explore its possibilities:

- Blackflies: Two steps out of my house and I was assaulted by blackflies, little flies that breed in streams of fast-running water and make outdoor living a kind of nuisance in the month of June. My question: What is their function? Nature has a reason. What is it?
- Ants: We've had black ants in our home for the first time. I witness them in large numbers in the garden in front of our home, poking their way over bark shavings and heading for the house. Hmm. Why do they want to come inside?
- House across the valley: All year long I look at several homes across the valley. I know them in each of the seasons, yet I've never met the people inside. My question: Who are those people? Can I construct them, build the person from the house?
- Devil's paintbrush: A bright red and yellow flower on the bank sloping away from our house. Why is it given that name?
- Unknown flower: There is a purple wildflower that goes up the stalk with tiny petals that cluster like grapes on an arbor. As they ascend up the stalk they go four across. I don't know its name but I want to understand it more. How can I learn more?
- Birch trees on the edge of the wood: Two birch trees look so healthy because the timber above them has been cut away and now their leaves get an abundance of light. It is as if they have been removed from jail and given windows on the world. What has happened?
- New growth on stumps: I've noticed this before, but the leaves on stalks that come from stumps are three to four times their normal size. I'd guess that the entire root system for a large tree is now delivering nutrition to just a few leaves. There is a teaching metaphor here; what is it?
- Dog pee: Our female dog pees in a puddle. The grass in the center dies on impact but the grass on the sides grows

richer and better. What's going on here? Why is it richer and such a lovely deep green in color?

- The sound of motorcycles: Amid the sound of a southwest wind through the aspen leaves as they sway back and forth I hear the growl of motorcycles down on Route 16 in the valley. Such a constrast. Such ambivalence within me. What does it mean?
- Coralbells: One sprig of coralbells blooming on the edge of the lawn, waving back and forth in the breeze like a red semaphore saying, "Over here, over here." Do flowers beckon? Never thought of that.

There, that's my list of notes. I'll take two items from the list and see what kind of poem may be there. Many poems begin this way—with an itch, an observation, a question, or a hunch that something might be there. There is something in the corner of my mind that I'll run with to see what happens.

I'll choose the stump with the large leaves. I see the stump in my mind's eye and that's all. A stump and a simple question, "How come?" What's there? I'll admit straightaway that I am a little afraid that there is nothing more than the question I've written. Even these few sentences I've just written may be a way of delaying out of fear that nothing is there. So, I'll start to write and, above all, to play a little.

> *A bristly stump*
> *filled with the fingers*
> *of new growth*
> *and leaves the size*
> *of panda ears*
> *springs saucy*
> *and vibrant*
> *into a new year;*
> *last year a crash*
> *and thump to the ground*
> *the snarling chain saw*

leveling ground
for the new house,
an interloper from down
country who claimed
the ground for a nest
high on the mountainside,
but over the winter
resolutions sprung deep
life in bunkers, sleeping
but waiting for the spring
offensive, meals that shoot
up the dumb waiter
for the light above ground;
a first green spring,
then a beachhead claimed
thrusting above the snow,
then a bud, now a leaf,
then the full broad leaves,
the first leaves
rich green, broad and flat
the full tree below
ground sending all those
loud messages of new life
to the interlopers.

I'll stop there. I can feel the images petering out. Still, there are a few lines and images I like here. Not much more. The notions of the tree starting out anew, borne from winter resolutions, and the huge tree that exists underground are important to me. The notion of some kind of struggle from below is something to work with again. Richard Lattimore (1972) writes in his poem "It" "a poem is a 'not-yet.' " And indeed it is. Some rapid sketching in words, the lines coming from heaven knows where, a kind of listening to the pictures and the questions in my head, the answers written in a column as new images and questions roll down the page. I'll work with it again.

A day later, I've tied into something complex with this poem, so complex that I turn to prose to free myself from the limitations imposed by line breaks. Here are my further musings about the stump:

Cut off the head and the body still lives. Hundreds of feet of roots don't know there isn't any head and that the tree above is gone.

New shoots thrust their way up from the stump. Cut off the tree and you get two new shoots that branch into seven, then fourteen— branching and reaching up, the nourishment pouring in from below.

Take away the head of an organization and deep down structure pours life into new veins, new branching. It doesn't result in the tree that came before but it does result in quick branches.

You can't take away a leader like Nelson Mandela and suddenly have the same kind of leadership. I saw that thin, wispy man and I wonder how, after twenty-seven years in prison, that frail body, despite his vibrant spirit, withstood such a demanding trip to New York and other cities. If he goes, then how can he be replaced? His support runs deep, but if he goes I fear a crisis in leadership.

I don't know if that bit of prose will work. The stump, the new shoots, are some kind of metaphor for the leadership problem. Of course, the metaphor may not be sound. I'll work on it again.

I'll try one more poem from my notes, this time about the coralbells:

> *Took a walk down*
> *the driveway heading*
> *for the splay*
> *of red and orange portulacas*
> *celebrating afta-shave*

in the morning sun;
a thin, reedy voice
poked in from my left;
"hey, over here;
how come you never come
over here," a gangly
slip of red coralbells
stood, reaching and resolute
on the edge of a great
drop of wall,
a cheeky devil
in lipstick and gangly
earrings demanding
her lonely place.

I like the idea that some flowers feel left out and claim their place. When I made my list for poems outdoors I remembered the coralbell, all alone on the edge of the wall, one bit of color in a new garden. But the remembering didn't come until I started the poem. Indeed, that sprig of red bells seemed to be calling out, pealing out. The poem is a rough cut, but I feel good about flowers that have personalities, beckon, and demand their place. I'll probably work with this idea again.

CORALBELLS

Took a walk
down the driveway
heading for a splash
of portulacas
celebrating afta-shave
in the morning sun;

a reedy voice poked
in from my left,
"hey over here;
look over here;

> *how come you never come*
> *over here," one thin,*
> *wispy slip of coralbells*
> *stood, reaching and resolute*
> *on the edge of a great drop*
> *of wall, a cheeky devil*
> *in lipstick and gangly*
> *earrings demanding*
> *her rightful place*
> *in the yard.*

This poem was much easier to write than "Stump." The issue or point emerged simply and quickly. The rewrite was merely a mopping up. I may do a little more work on the words over the next few weeks, but the point I wanted to make seems to have been made.

ACTION: GO OUTSIDE, FIND SOME POEMS, AND DO SOME ROUGH DRAFTS.

Go alone. Carry a notepad and write down the various questions or phenomena—the itches—that interest you. If others are involved, agree that you will not talk until after you have finished your lists. Above all make your own observations. To some degree you may find this trip similar to a science field trip. At least, that's what happened to me. If I had run with the notion of motorcycles buzzing in the valley I would have been into noise pollution. There were no people around when I went outside this time but I might have picked up on some observations of human behavior.

I work principally from pictures, the coralbells off to the side or the broad leaves of the new maple on the stump. Words follow the pictures, digging their way into meaning. I watch and record, letting my mind run uncensored through a first draft. Sound creeps in to help the sense, as in "filled with the fingers."

How the lines go down remains something of a mystery to

me, although there are a few things I attempt to do in a first draft. The words may flow in long lines if I want the poem to feel as if it is carrying weight. Short, staccato lines may emphasize more rapid, biting motion.

I try to end each line with a strong verb or noun. For example, ending with *of, to, and,* or an adjective would weaken the line. This is not a rule, just a general guideline. There are no rules other than to aim for a desired effect and the sense I wish to convey.

I also try to write with strong verbs and nouns, making each precise enough to rule out unnecessary adverbs and adjectives. An extra adverb may mean I was propping up a tired verb; the same is true for adjectives and nouns. These concerns, however, I save for fine-tuning in later drafts.

ACTION: SEND CHILDREN OUTSIDE TO FIND SOME POEMS.

So much of what the children will see outdoors is connected with how you approach your curriculum. "How come?" "Why did that happen?" "Can you speculate on the meaning of that?" These questions ought to be common parlance in your classroom. They are the words of the poet as much as the scientist. Poets see connections everywhere. They allow no walls to exist between disparate data. They delight in paradox.

Send your small poets' group out into the schoolyard in teams of two. Ask them to try some of the following:

- Find something very small that you have never looked at closely before. Describe it.
- Find something growing. How is it growing?
- Find something broken. How did it get broken?
- Look for people. What are they doing? How are they using the outdoors?
- Find something and ask, "Suppose this didn't exist. What then?"

- Sit very quietly for two minutes. List all the sounds you hear.
- Feel the weather touch you, first with your eyes open, then with your eyes closed. What did you feel? What do you wonder about?

Send the children out prepared for surprises, for rumination, for wondering. Send them out prepared to see and record detail. Good questions come from details that don't make sense, that make us speculate. A short discussion will help children to prepare their minds to wonder and question. My final word to the children: "Perhaps you will see something you have never seen before. Maybe you will think a brand new thought or come up with a surprise question." I stress the individuality of their observation. If it is new to you, that is all that counts.

ACTION: CONSIDER THE PERIPHERY OF THOUGHT.

Donald Murray has taught me to trust the shadows. In general, I'm a goal-oriented person. I wear blinders, keeping my head focused on the objective. All my efforts point toward the end of the tunnel, the light where I can pause and say, "Mission accomplished." A sense of focus is essential in learning to write. I hear the voices of my teachers, "An article, novel, or poem can only be about one thing." Correct advice, but I have often interpreted their words in bulldog fashion: "Choose a focus and don't waver."

That decision rules out discovery and risks losing the rich ideas that can be hovering on the periphery, in the shadows of the mind, waiting to come into the mainstream. I have to admit that only in recent years have the shadows meant anything to me. First I had to realize that there is "real stuff" there.

"Shadows" and "periphery" need explaining. Writing is a way of seeing, first for myself then for others. But my primary focus is my own seeing. When I look out the window of my upstairs study in the mountains of New Hampshire, I see North and South Doublehead mountains, along with Chandler and Black mountains. In my study I note the edge of a tapestry of rising hot-air balloons on my right side and a scene of two cranes on a silk-screened background on my left. I probe for a connection between the mountains and these two peripheral scenes and realize that the outdoors is so much a part of my life, I have surrounded myself with it, inside and outside.

But the periphery could just as easily have been a metaphor, a new idea, or a new connection to something I see or hear. I watch the edges and listen. *Listen* is a critical word here. I get used to trusting my own vision by putting that vision to the test. Faith is not blind; it is borne of a long history of trusting the results of my daily writing. I mine the past and present, knowing that, usually, something is there.

ACTION: WRITE TO BRING IN THE PERIPHERY.

In this Action you will write rapidly about an event. Although you have done this before, this time you will write rapidly enough to deliberately bring in the periphery of your vision, whether things you see, or new connections or ideas. I will do the exercise with you. First, since I have nothing in my mind at the moment, I'll take a short look at yesterday and make a list of what is there.

- Birthday cake.
- David's home.
- Falling asleep listening to a ball game.
- Visit from the Allens.
- Looking over movies.
- The Sunday paper.
- A look for the beavers.

Not until I wrote down my final item did I sense that there might be a poem in any of the events. Our trip to see beavers at work ended in a dead end. I'll compose rapidly, allowing the periphery to take hold, although at the moment I only have the picture of the beaver pond in my mind's eye and one single question, "What happened?"

I stole
down the steep bank
peering through the aspens
and criss-cross underbrush,
poking a hole through the curtain
of underbrush for one quick glimpse
of beaver, the aftertrail
of their wake making a way
to the thatched-twigged home
on the bank beneath the hemlock
one last look before a child's
shout or dog's bark
chased them to shelter.

But the pond lay deep and dark
with the tannin of trees
the chestnut amber
the dripping of quiet water
from the dam still intact
but there were no beaver
no fresh cut shavings
just the yellowed remnants
of April's chewing
no fresh prints in dam mud
only the shouts of children
prancing and slipping
on old logs midst their
wonderings and questions,
"Will they come out now,
grandpa?"

I have to admit that it is a little difficult to know periphery from center. I certainly wasn't conscious of one or the other while I was writing. I was merely "letting in" what was there without censoring. Now I'll go back and note some of the "yeses" that were new and surprising to me. I call "new" a periphery.

> *poking a hole through the curtain of underbrush*
> *the aftertrail of their wake*
> *tannin of trees*
> *dripping of quiet water*
> *children prancing and slipping*

These pictures were new to me. I didn't know they were there until I let them in during the writing. They came as if I'd set a video camera in slow forward position. As I reread the lines there is a feeling of anticipation, then the reality that the beavers are no longer there and the children no longer quiet. But even as I write these words, there is still more on the periphery in the form of questions that demand new information:

- Did the game warden shoot the beavers as the owner had asked?
- Why was the dam still intact?
- Is my evidence correct? No new shavings or trees down means they are dead?

Questions are like reels that pull information out of murky water. During this entire process I am listening only to myself, my questions . . . and I am trusting my listening because the questions seem right to me. These are crude words, these first words trying to find a poem, but they are words on which I know I can build. The tone will be one of sadness, I suspect. I will write to recapture those feelings—first for myself and then for the reader.

ACTION: FIND A POEM IN THE EVENTS OF THE LAST TWENTY-FOUR HOURS.

As part of your participation in this Action, make a list of events from yesterday. No matter how insignificant, list them to see what is there. Form a question about each one, a question like, "So what's the meaning of that?" Then, with the question in your head, write rapidly, changing nothing but showing the event and the items (people, things) involved in the event. Let whatever lies shyly at the edge of your mind come into the poem. Don't try to integrate it, just let it in, but let it in as clearly as you can. Try this for five minutes.

ACTION: WRITE PROSE FROM A POEM.

This morning I've written a poem that isn't working very well. I'm uneasy about the first draft. I won't abandon it just yet but, as an experiment, I'll write the same incident in prose. The prose may help my poem, or the poem may help my prose. These genres exist to make meaning. Let me explain what I mean.

Last Saturday I witnessed a near-devastating accident on Interstate 95. The experience was filled with such emotion and perplexity on my part that I kept asking, "What does all this mean? Why have I been so affected?" I thought there might be a poem there. I usually turn to poetry when I am most puzzled by events. Here is my first draft:

ACCIDENT

Interstate 95 north,
Sweet Georgia Brown
and Canadian Brass
bounce a beat
from the deck,
two black strips
with green in between,
music and the open road.

Dirt spurts
like smoke,
a fountain of dust
like strafing bullets

chewing paths
on a country road;
from those plumes,
a confusion
of red on green,
a veering Subaru,
hiccuping the median
then somersaulting
like an Olympian
in triple jump, once,
twice, and thrice
but on cue
a body ejects
like Ringling
would be proud,
a long arch
to the ground;
I replay now
in slow motion,
the body racing
ahead of the car,
then bouncing
and halting to rest,
but the car
coming, rolling,
searching for the lost
master, ready
to crush the master.

I stop,
hit the flashers
race the highway,
sprint the median,
the car now an ugly
red beetle upside down,

the engine in fury
poops smoke, the wheels
race and paw the empty
air. Two men
cradle a young woman
racing from the car,
"Might blow up,
get her out of here.
anyone else in there?
she's the only one."
"How can I get to Medford?"
asks the girl.

Unlike most first drafts, this one did not go down quickly. I kept replaying the incident in my mind's eye. I'd guess it took me about half an hour of stopping and starting to get it down. To some degree I am suspicious of pieces that go too slowly; that's my style. Halfway through I said to myself, "I'm not sure this is a poem." I'll see if it works better in prose. I am confident that the poem will help my prose. Let's see what happens.

I was heading north on Interstate 95, a four-lane highway separated from the southbound lane with a three-hundred-foot-wide grass divider strip. I was doing 70 while listening to "Sweet Georgia Brown" played by the Canadian Brass on my tape deck.

I caught a puff of what looked like smoke off to my left in the southbound lane. Suddenly there were spurts of "smoke," which I soon realized were spurts of dirt flung high into the air by a braking car. Suddenly the car, a red Subaru, was bouncing across the grassy divider with some possibility of coming all the way over into the northbound lane. I veered to the right. At that moment, the Subaru veered crazily and began a series of rolls, then end to end flips. On the second flip, a body ejected from the car, catapulting ahead of the car and onto the ground. My recall suggests that the whole event lasted longer than it did.

I suspect that three seconds elapsed from the time the Subaru left the highway for the median until I had gone by. My last picture of the scene was of an inert person lying on the ground with the car rolling toward her/him.

I stopped my car, tapped the four-way flasher button, and sprinted across the highway. By now about twenty to thirty cars had stopped. As I sprinted down the median, I met two men carrying a girl, half running and walking away from the car. "Got to get her away from the car; it might blow up," said one of the men.

The car was upside down, a kind of ungainly beetle trying desperately to right itself. The engine was racing and pouring smoke from the exhaust, the tires spinning purposelessly in the air. The men were right, the gasoline tank might have ruptured and with all that heat being generated with the running engine, blow sky high.

My first thought was that the girl they were carrying was a passenger in the car. "Any others?" I asked. "Nope, she's the one." They sat her down on the ground where I first met them, satisfied that the distance was sufficiently safe from her auto that was still running upside down with the threat of an imminent explosion.

She was a young woman of about twenty-two years. She sat on the grass shaking her head and crying slightly, not from pain but more from the loss of her car. Her shoulder was scraped and she complained of pain in her lower right leg when the medic, recently arrived, tried to move it. He sent his assistant back to the van to get a splint. I was afraid of shock. Her face didn't show it, but I wasn't sure if internal injuries might not suddenly come into play and she'd be in quick trouble. "Better have her head be in the right position for shock," I said. (This was before the medics arrived. I was surprised that they were more interested in her leg injury than the possibility of shock.)

The girl began to speak, "Oh, my car, my car."

"Don't worry about your car," said one of her carriers, "you are here and alive."

"Okay, but how am I going to get to Medford?" was her next question.

I wondered if her near escape from death was something she'd ever remember. I wondered if she'd ever recall her flight through the air, bouncing off the ground with the car rolling toward her, and threatening to crush her.

I have my doubts about this piece. It is more of a chronicle of what happened, with some influence from the poem but not nearly as much as I'd expected. I'm wondering if there isn't an essay underneath. There isn't any great question rumbling inside me—at least that I am conscious of. I need to think about the questions underlying the writing. I'll make a list here. That may help me with both poetry and prose.

- How was it possible for her to escape serious injury, flying through the air as she did?
- People really do stop to help others. In the space of three to four minutes at least twenty to thirty cars had stopped. Some were curious but most came to help and at some danger to themselves. (Two men crawled inside the window and turned off the car engine.)
- I am more impressed by the design of the highways than ever before. The width of the median is critical as well as the pitch of the median, which first pitched down and then up and therefore offered protection to travelers on the opposite side of the highway.
- At any second, cars traveling at high speed can go out of control and only seconds separate you at any time from instant death and serious injury.
- How well-prepared am I to help another injured person? I regret that my knowledge of first aid is so thin. Something to think about.
- Peripheral vision and its rapid translation are essential survival tools. In fact, significant occasions are usually at

the edge of thought or vision. They serve as early warning systems or elements of prospective delight.

As I write down these questions and observations I realize that my uneasiness about both the poem and the short prose piece may be connected with the notion that no writing can do justice to the event. At this point I am more inclined to write an essay with some focus on a particular point. My report of the accident is dry and uneventful. However, this exercise does show how much of an event can be compressed in just a few lines of poetry. The prose is longer and more convoluted. Poetry, on the other hand, is arranged to get at the essence of something.

For this Action try writing a narrative account based on one of your poems. Perhaps this will work better for you than it did for me. The objective in doing this Action is to get the feel of different genres in relation to each other. Some ideas work best as essays, others as narrative or fiction, and still others as poetry. There may be a few occasions when you may find it helpful to nudge some of your best writers into writing about one event in several different genres.

ACTION: CONSIDER REVISING A POEM YOU HAVE WRITTEN QUICKLY.

I revise poems because the first words I write don't always say what I mean. Of course, what I think I mean is only a hunch at first. Take the poem "Accident," which initially I didn't like at all. I wrote a first draft and cared so little for it that I thought I'd work on a narrative or essay instead. My poor narrative drove me back to the poem because the accident as event still perplexed me. The words, "What happened anyway?" kept going through my mind. And when I read the first draft to a few others, they thought it had promise. When I finally reached some state of finality, I realized that some of the changes I made might be instructive.

Before I wrote the poem I decided that the lines would be short. Since there was high drama and lots of motion, the short lines would connote speed. I also decided that I'd simply tell the story using the natural order of events—driving down the highway, seeing the accident, stopping my car, and racing to where the person was on the ground. I wrote each part just as I witnessed the elements of the accident. This approach is called "following natural order."

Figure 7–1 shows the first draft of the poem and, on the right, my critical comments. The comments will show what I will work on in draft 2.

I'm a little surprised that I've made so many statements about words and their lack of precision. On the other hand, until the words have more precision, I won't know what I intend to say. Sections 1, 2, and 3 make me uneasy. I'll rewrite them.

Note that I deliberately make favorable comments about what I like and about lines that create "right" feelings and pictures. The good lines and precise pictures are elements on which I can build; they give the poem a foundation. I am still working toward precise pictures. After I realize more clearly what I have discovered, I will probably see how to organize the poem better.

More changes came in the next draft (Figure 7–2). I didn't put in all the changes I'd recommended from draft 1. Sometimes there is simply more to do than can be done in one new draft. The minute I make new changes other problems emerge. This is quite normal. Until I can straighten out one section and make the meaning more clear to myself, I can't see some of the other nagging problems. Three major shifts occurred here:

- The description of the car needed to come after the body rolling and the car searching for the body.
- I need to leave the poem and let the poem focus just on the accident itself. I'm not sure about taking myself out of the beginning of the poem.
- The poem is far too long. I look for the one line that says what the poem is about (something I do much more now) and I find it in the last line: "How am I going to get to

FIGURE 7–1   FIRST DRAFT OF POEM WITH CRITICAL COMMENTS

```
            Accident
Interstate 95 north,
Sweet Georgia Brown
and Canadian Brass
       ce
bound a beat
from the deck,
two black strips
with green in between,
music and the open road.

Dirt spurts
like smoke,
a fountain of dust
like strafing bullets
chewing paths
on a country road;
from those plumes,
a confusion
of red on green,
a veering Subaru,
hiccuping the median
then somersaulting
like an Olympian
in triple jump, once,
```

OK, I need to show what the accident interrupted.

#1 } This bothers me, but it is here because I thought the reader needed to know the highway was a dual lane.

ι too prosaic

I like the sudden, abrupt start and short lines
• Too many likes
"Fountain" connotes too much peace.

good line

→ again a soft word

key "conf

I like the bouncy "hiccup" but I don't think it works

OK.

FIGURE 7-1 (CONTINUED)

twice, and thrice
but on cue
a body ejects
like Ringling
would be proud,
a long arch
to the ground;
I replay now
in slow motion,
the body racing
ahead of the car,
then bouncing
and halting to rest,
but the car
coming, rolling,
searching for the lost
master, ready
to crush the master.

#2
This is much too long,
but I had to get it
all down.

see
#2

I stop,
hit the flashers
race the highway,
sprint the median,

FIGURE 7–1　(CONTINUED)

the car now an ugly
red beetle upside down,　　}　I like this part.
the engine in fury
poops smoke, the wheels
race and paw the empty　　　paw — tires don't paw.
air.　Two men
cradle a young woman　　　Can't tell who races
racing from the car,
"might blow up,　　　　　}　#3
get her out of here.　　　　　a little
anyone else in there　　　　too much
she's the only one."　　　　dialogue
"How can I get to Medford?"　　I like this line - key.
asks the girl.

FIGURE 7–2   SECOND DRAFT OF POEM WITH CRITICAL COMMENTS

Accident

Interstate 95 north,
Sweet Georgia Brown
and Canadian Brass
bounce a beat
from the deck,
music and the open road.

Good, but do I belong in the poem here?

(I removed black strips with green.)

Dirt spurts
like smoke,
a fountain of dust
like strafing bullets
chewing paths
on a country road;
from those brown
plumes, a confusion
of red on green,
a Subaru veers
the median then vaults
in triple somersault,
like an olympian
once, twice, and on cue
a body ejects like Ringling
would be proud
a long arch
to the ground;
I replay now
in slow motion,
the body rolls
ahead of the car,
which searches
for its master.

still not right.

more active than veering — good.

good verb

rolls – more accurate than races

I've lost the grim struggle

FIGURE 7–2   (CONTINUED)

I stop,
hit the flashers
race the highway,
sprint the median,
two men scoop a body
off the ground,
the car an ugly
beetle upside down,
the engine in fury
poops smoke,
its wheels race
and scrape the empty
air.

I don't belong in The poem.

This is in The wrong place.

I like scrape juxtaposed c̄ empty air.

Two men cradle
the body, a woman
whose face bawls
bewilderment, "might
blow up, get her
out of here."
"anyone else in there?"
"she's the only one,"
"how am I going
to get to Medford?"
asks the woman.

I like the bawling, but she was in a stunned kind-of-bewilderment. Got to fix That.

still too wordy

better – Sara Blake helped here.

Medford?" I need to focus more on the woman, and I need to get to her more quickly.

Three drafts later the poem reads this way:

INTERSTATE 95 NORTH

A Subaru veers
the median
a panic of red
on green, then vaults
an olympic triple
somersault, once,
twice, a body ejects
a long, flopping arch
to the ground;
the body rolls
ahead of the car,

Now a sprawled
beetle on its back;
the engine exhausts
gouts of black smoke;
the wheels race
and whine in the empty air.

Two men scoop the body
from the ground,
"Might blow up,"
shouts one;
they race and cradle
the woman whose eyes blink
as if the light
is too much for her.
She asks, "How am I going
to get to Medford?"

I will now review a number of guidelines I followed in writing and revising the poem:

- I write rapidly, listening to and observing the event as I write. I play with words, knowing that I will come back to revise. How I write the first draft has everything to do with how I will continue to revise.
- I can't make all the revisions in one draft.
- I keep in touch with what I like in a poem as well as what makes me uneasy.
- In this poem, I should have looked for the line I thought showed what the poem was about much earlier than I did.
- Once I discover what the poem is about, I struggle with the universal element it touches on.
- I decide what lines have most to do with the one line the poem is about and get rid of the others. (Some of the deleted lines may be good lines, but wave goodbye to them nevertheless. The more conviction you have about what the poem is about, the easier it is to delete what the poem is not about.)
- I double-check *verbs*. They, more than the other words, are the engine of poetry.

ACTION: TRY SOME APPROACHES TO REVISING ONE OF THE POEMS YOU CARE ABOUT.

Take five minutes and do some of the following:

- *Verbs:* Underline all the verbs in your poem. Change the verbs that need it so they are more active and precise.
- *Ends of lines:* Examine the verbs and nouns at the ends of lines. Are those the principal words you use at the ends of lines? Beware of prepositions, conjunctions, adjectives, and adverbs. Also, remember that in all art there are exceptions, but the exceptions are not accidental. They are often

deliberate and contribute to a deeper meaning or a sense of surprise.

- *The one line:* Draw a line under *the one line* that says most what you want the poem to be about. If you have to amend a line to make it the most important line, then do it.
- *Add:* Look over your poem to decide how you will enhance other lines so they complement the one line you've chosen.
- *Delete:* Get rid of the lines that do not complement your one important line.

A TEACHER BEGINS TO WRITE POETRY   Lisa Noble is a teacher intern in the Master of Arts Teaching program at the University of New Hampshire. Although she has written some poetry in the past, she recently concentrated on her poetry and reflected on the process. I want to share Lisa's poetry and her reflections because she is beginning to think as a poet thinks about the world. Her questions are questions of meaning: "Why?" "What's the truth about that?" "What's the meaning of that?" "What's the best way to capture the meaning and the feeling?"

Lisa writes about her cat as it walks on the table in front of her. Here is the first stanza of the poem:

> *Jenny, a cat*
> *deep dark velvet black*
> *slides by*
> *pushing the corner of my book with*
> *her forehead*
> *her chin*
> *her cheek.*
> *Tail high*
> *back arched to its limit*
> *Meowing.*
> *A desperate call.*

Lisa's comments in her journal show that she has discovered poetry in the everyday:

There could be more detail in this poem but all that it is doing (its purpose for existing) is to give an image. Really nothing more. I wrote the poem as it happened. I was sitting at my kitchen table trying to study and Jenny would not leave me alone. So, I wrote about it. I enjoy writing poetry like this. In fact, almost every time I sit down I think of something to write about.

Although Lisa is dismissing her short poem as somewhat offhand and possibly trivial, she is doing the rapid sketching, the simple showing, so vital to the work of a poet. She is downright pleased with the feeling she knows from writing about the cat. She should be. Although she might work on line breaks and precision of language, she begins with such a strong verb, *slides*, that she is able to build a poem on this one word.

Lisa goes on to write about tougher stuff, the feelings she has (or doesn't have) for a young man. She goes through many drafts trying to show just how she feels about him, although the feelings are so complicated it takes a number of drafts just to probe through to what she actually thinks. She uses the concise space of a poem—and an even more compressed space within the poem—to come to terms with their relationship.

Sittings
my hands folded through my arms
Nodding
your stomach tight under my bony rear
I reach down stroke your face

lost
i am lost

somewhere between our walk along the river
   on the frozen ground
      listening to the tide crackle and creak
      as it came under the ice
and our work on the sailplane
      you have so affectionately named grumpy

> *i left my body*
> *worse than that, I left my soul.*
> *the writer*
> *the thinker*
> *the wonderer*
> *Gone.*
>
> *The touch of my hand to your face is empty.*
> *I try to drain the energy back*
> *but fail,*
> *I'm*
> *lost.*

Lisa comments on her first draft, slightly embarrassed by her first attempt (sharing a first draft is akin to having someone rudely open the door while you are partially dressed).

I wrote this, saved it on the computer, and then read it to a friend a couple of days later. When I read the poem I realized that I didn't like "lost, i am lost." Nor did I like "i left my body," worse than that, "I left my soul." In fact I was embarrassed reading them out loud. I knew they had to be changed. The question was: what did I really mean by those words? What did I want the reader to know at that point?

I did like the description of me sitting on his stomach and the description of the tide coming in under the ice. Those things needed to stay. I also liked how there was action (my touching his face) and within that split second, I have the thoughts contained in the second stanza.

Lisa went to work again and experimented, starting with the "touch of her hand" in the first version. She tries to show on paper some hunches she has about her feelings:

> *The hungry touch of my hand to your face*
> *encounters*
>   *emptiness*

I want the energy given so freely
  trusting that it would be
    digested transformed given back

My hands come away
empty
tearing through the empty air
reaching, gripping my cold cheeks
tearing skin
imagining bone
desperate for my energy back.

wetness
  a tear
    wandering down the smallest finger
    on my wrist
      it drops off my elbow
        falls to the floor.

Lisa sticks her neck out and is both surprised and dismayed by what she sees. She tried to give flesh to the emotion through words. She comments on what she has done:

The part about losing myself is still not good. It is amost too clear. I am telling the reader too much. I am just repeating the obvious. But, the poem won't be confused for a love poem anymore. (Although it is about love, "love poems" usually imply something positive.) The anger that I felt is appearing in the poem and although I didn't really tear my skin (in fact only the walk and the sailplane really happened), the image gets across the feelings I want—desperation, solitude, anger, sadness, emptiness. The second to last stanza is pretty dramatic and scary. Do I really want it that way? This is a problem that I face often in my writing. I don't want to write down some of the images that I see. They seem too violent to be coming out of someone who is supposed to be calm. I haven't learned to trust that part of myself yet.

Although Lisa has been working at writing poetry for a very short time, she is attending to many of the features poets are concerned about:

• Specifics.
• The match between specifics and feelings.
• Coming to terms with a new self that is going public.
• The feel of a line.
• The necessity of experimenting on the page (in the head is not the same as on the page).

Lisa's latest draft of her poem is the following:

sitting
my hands folded through my arms
listening, nodding
your stomach tight under my bony rear
i reach down to stroke your face

somewhere between our walk along the river
      on the frozen crusted ground
      listening to the tide crackle and creak
      as it groaned in under the ice
and our work on the sailplane
      you so affectionately named "grumpy"
I lost
writerthinkerwonderer

the hungry touch of my hand to your face
encounters emptyness
the energy given so freely
      trusting that it would be digested, transformed given back
was absorbed

my hand comes away
tears through static air
reaches, grips cold cheeks

pierces skin
imagines bone.

Lisa looks back on her brief experience as a poet:

So, in my brief life as a poet (or at least of seeing myself as a poet),
I have seen myself grow from nonspecific to more specific and I am
now attempting to apply specifics to more general emotional issues.
    The exciting part about knowing about my own growth as a
writer is that it comes in handy in the classroom. Just yesterday
I worked with a student on her poetry. She was having trouble
describing exactly what she meant. She was writing in generalities.
Because I had experienced the problem, I could pull out my own
drafts of poetry and show her what I did. This way she could see a
poet besides herself in action. She could see the difference between
the first draft and the final product. But, most importantly, she
could talk to me as one writer to another and as one reader to
another. We could then have a conversation on her poetry and how
she was going to form the next draft. I can't wait to see what she
comes up with.

Lisa has come full circle, from working with her own poetry
to helping a student in her eighth-grade classroom. Lisa's confidence in her own growth as a poet as well as her awareness
of the process of writing poetry prepared her to help the student. She sees the importance of her writing when, as she says,
the student "could talk to me as one writer to another and as
one reader to another." The depth of Lisa's teaching in this
instance is governed by the seriousness of her own writing. She
writes poetry for herself, not on behalf of the student. And that
makes all the difference.

FINAL REFLECTION   You have continued your own exploration of poetry by going
outdoors and by being more sensitive to the periphery of your
thinking to allow images and notions into your poetry that you

may have excluded in the past. Although you have continued to experiment with rapid, five- to ten-minute exercises, you now revise by considering the verbs, the ends of lines, the one line the poem is about, and the addition and deletion of information.

8

choral speaking
and the learning of poems

Choral speaking is one of the best ways to share in poetry's sounds and shadings of meaning as a group. Sheila Tetelson (Chapter 6) begins her year with choral speaking. She has found it an important way to build class spirit and share the joy of a common language repertoire.

There is no more rapid way for children to learn and enjoy a poem than through choral speaking. It is not unusual for first- and second-grade children to learn two poems a week. This chapter is designed to help you move into choral speaking in your classroom. I have chosen poems that lend themselves to choral speaking; and I will share some ways you can help children memorize the poems, and some methods I have found helpful in leading children in choral speaking.

Before moving into the details, try reading some of the following poems aloud. Read each one at least three times, then choose two you'd like to use in working with the children.

ACTION: READ THE FOLLOWING POEMS ALOUD AND CHOOSE TWO YOU LIKE FOR CHORAL SPEAKING.

THE PASTURE SPRING

I'm going out to clean the pasture spring;
I'll only stop to rake the leaves away
(And wait to watch the water clear, I may):
I sha'n't be gone long. —You come too.

I'm going out to fetch the little calf.
That's standing by the mother. It's so young
It totters when she licks it with her tongue.
I sha'n't be gone long. —You come too.

Robert Frost

THE PICKETY FENCE

The pickety fence
The pickety fence
Give it a lick it's

143

The pickety fence
Give it a lick it's
A clickety fence
Give it a lick it's
A lickety fence
Give it a lick
Give it a lick
Give it a lick
With a rickety stick
Pickety
Pickety
Pickety
Pick.

David McCord

AROUND AND AROUND

The flower's on the bird
Which is underneath the bee
And the bird is on the kitten
On the cat on me
I'm on a chair
On some grass
On a lawn
And the lawn is on a meadow
And the world is what it's on
And all of us together
When the day is nearly done
Like to sit and watch the weather
As we spin around the sun.

Karla Kuskin

THE MEAL

Timothy Tompkins had turnips and tea.
The turnips were tiny.
He ate at least three.

And then, for dessert,
He had onions and ice.
He liked that so much
That he ordered it twice.
He had two cups of ketchup,
A prune, and a pickle.
"Delicious," said Timothy.
"Well worth a nickel."
He folded his napkin
And hastened to add,
"It's one of the loveliest breakfasts I've had."

Karla Kuskin

NOT ME

The Slithergadee has crawled out of the sea
He may catch all the others, but he won't catch me.
No you won't catch me, old Slithergadee,
You may catch all the others, but you wo . . .

Shel Silverstein

ON LEARNING TO ADJUST TO THINGS

Baxter Bickerbone of Burlington
Used to be sheriff till he lost his gun.
Used to be a teacher till he lost his school.
Used to be an iceman till he lost his cool.
Used to be a husband till he lost his wife.
Used to be alive till he lost his life.
When he got to heaven Baxter said,
"The climate's very healthy once you're used to being dead."

John Ciardi

WINDY NIGHTS

Rumbling in the chimneys,
Rattling at the doors,
Round the roofs and round the roads
The rude wind roars;

> *Raging through the darkness,*
> *Raving through the trees,*
> *Racing off again across*
> *The great grey seas.*
>
> Rodney Bennett

ACTION: LEARN SOME POEMS.

My memories of learning poetry are not pleasant. "I'd like you to memorize this poem by Friday." The dreaded words were spoken. We knew that in seventh grade memorizing poetry was a requirement. The eighth graders had warned us, "Sometime around Christmas you'll have to memorize Alfred Noyes's 'The Highwayman.'" I'd already peeked at the poem, considered the length, and hoped it wouldn't ruin my Christmas holiday. I recall that learning the poem was a triumph, like climbing a mountain. Arriving breathless at the summit, I was amazed that the human mind, especially mine, could accomplish such a feat as recalling the precise words of a poet.

The poem didn't become part of me until years later. In fact, not until much later in life, say thirty years, have I come to appreciate how important it is to carry poetry with me through memorization. Walking down a street, sitting by a lake, waiting in an airport terminal, I can turn over the beauty of a poem and what it represents just by saying it to myself. Best of all, in saying the poem I can continually discover new meanings in the poem itself.

Back in seventh grade I didn't have help in learning the poem. It loomed in front of me like a boulder that needed splitting and removing. So I'd like to suggest some approaches to learning the poems you have chosen that have worked for me. If you already have a system that works for you, then use it.

You will need to learn a poem to work with choral speaking in class. I'll take the easiest first, David McCord's "Pickety Fence." Try the following:

1. Read the poem aloud three times. I learn best through the ear. I hear songs, like them, and can whistle, sing, and hum them long before I know the words. I am caught first by the sound and rhythms. When I read "The Pickety Fence" I can feel the rhythm of a stick clicking along the vertical pickets as I walk along. Read the poem until you feel the rhythms of the stick on the pickets as you read aloud.

2. Once you have the feel of the sound and rhythm in the poem, look at the way the poem progresses, the way David McCord has structured it. There is the repeat of the refrain "the pickety fence" at the beginning; then the repeat of "Give it a lick" three times but with changing descriptors: pickety, clickety, lickety; then one more use of a new word, "rickety."

3. Now say the first three lines. Look away. Say the first three lines again, but unaided by the book. Now, feeling the rhythm of those first three lines, use your knowledge of how the author has put the poem together to try to say the poem as best you can right through to the end, inventing lines if you have to. Look back at how the poem is written again, noting any discrepancies between how the poem is written and how you said the poem. Work until you feel that the poem is a part of you, using rhythm and sense together to say it as David McCord has written it. Carry the poem with you for a few days; then teach the poem to the children.

ACTION: HELP CHILDREN TO ACQUIRE POEMS THROUGH CHORAL SPEAKING.

In choral speaking the children make the poem their own just as you did when you learned it by yourself. They learn it by experimenting with the sound and sense of the poem in the safety of the chorus of the entire class. They will not see the written poem, since they will learn it from you (this is why you learned it, the essential step in teaching poetry through choral speaking) by hearing it and doing their own experimentations. Here is a procedure that works for me:

1. Organize the class in front of you like a musical chorus. It is essential that all the children be able to see you, so group the taller members of the class at the back, the shorter ones in front. Stand not much more than eight feet back from the front row. Sometimes this will mean rearranging desks or moving to a part of the room that is more open. In a class of twenty-five, I'd arrange the children like this:

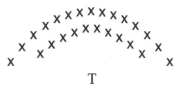

Sometimes I find it helpful to stand on a chair so the children can see me more easily.

2. Making sure that all eyes are on you, tell the children to watch your mouth as you say the poem through two times. Be sure to say it in such a way that you maintain the sound and sense. Do not slow down to help them learn it. The more you stay with the natural rhythm and meter, the more rapidly they will acquire and understand it.

3. Move just your lips and mouth, exaggerating the shape of the first two lines. At first you will want the children to focus on your mouth so they can read your lips as the class speaks the poem together. After they have said the first two lines with me silently, I ask them to speak the first two lines aloud. We do this two times before moving to the next step.

4. Tell the children to speak the poem. "Speak the parts you think you know. Just jump right in. Don't worry about making mistakes." I find it helpful to conduct the class with my hands. I'm not very good at it, but at least I get them to start together. The miracle of this approach is that two or three children know at least some part of the poem immediately. Even if the rest are a step behind, their errors can't be heard above the voices of the children who make it work. The class has become an immediate chorus.

5. Repeat, saying the poem together two or three times. Notice that I haven't gone over the meaning of the poem, discussed it, reviewed the structure, or given any analysis of it. I trust the poet's own sound and sense to teach the children when I have already memorized the poem before I start. I have learned the poem so that I can maintain eye contact with the children and observe them as they learn it.

6. Once most of the children have learned the poem after six to eight sayings over two days, I give them a copy of it. It is interesting to watch them note the complementary nature of what they would say and what is actually on the page. They can do final self-corrections on the full saying of the poem at this time. After all this, we may have a discussion of the poem, answering children's questions about the content or structure. Now we can do the fine-tuning on stress and volume in relation to the meaning of various parts of the poem.

Once the children have a repertoire of poems, they can say them anywhere: traveling on a field trip, waiting in line for buses or lunch or special events, filling in three minutes here and there. Choral speaking is one of the marvelous ways in which children become a group and everyone has a part. How easy it is in American education to focus so much on the individual that we lose the sense of collaborative power, the power of individuals who have a place in a group that is going somewhere and has a sense of self: "We can do these things." You can probably recall moments in your own education when you participated in a play, sang in a chorus or musicale, or played on a team. There was a joy in sensing the power of the group. Choral speaking enables us to have a sense of ourselves several times a day. Naturally, learning the possibilities of language, tasting sound and rhythm, and getting to know more poets are valuable carryovers as well.

9

*poetry belongs
throughout the curriculum*

Things are more than they seem. Beauty and paradox are every-where. I see an orange and black monarch butterfly alight on a yellow marigold. It is mid-September; the newspaper forecasts frost tonight. In my mind I scroll the knowledge that the monarch ought to have headed south before now, migrating thousands of miles home to a valley in Mexico where the species fills whole trees. An orange and black garden of butterflies. I worry that the monarch may not make it through the night's frost.

I observe the monarch systematically moving from floret to floret, dipping its proboscis to suck the marigold's nectar. When it is done, the monarch lifts a wing, rises from the floret, catches a thermal, and is gone to some new destination, I hope farther south.

This monarch is more than an insect in a textbook; it is more than body parts and habits. At once I am struck by its beauty in the garden, the miracle of its flight, its remarkable journey thousands of miles away, my own anxiety about the onset of an early frost. Such a mixture of admiration and personal involvement leads me quite naturally to combine poetry and science, aesthetics and hard facts. Poetry, probably more than any other kind of writing, allows me to combine all these feelings and facts in the short space of a few lines.

For too long we have believed the notion that science is quite separate from personal feelings. Somehow the scientist is the cold, calculating, objective human, distant from the normal emotions of ordinary beings. We have erred equally in the direction of saying that when we express feelings we do not need facts. Yet it is precisely my knowledge of the monarch's hazardous and lengthy migration that gives rise to my feelings about the butterfly.

One of my favorite poems, "The Bats," by Brendan Galvin, combines a great range of scientific and social data with wonder and admiration for another species.

THE BATS

Somebody said for killing one
you got a five-dollar reward
from Red Farrell the game warden,
because at night they drank cow blood,
dozens of them plastered on the cow
like leaves after a rain,
until she dropped.
If they bit you you'd get paralyzed for life,
and they built their nests
in women's hair, secreting goo
so you couldn't pull them out
and had to shave it off.
That was how Margaret Smith got bald,
though some said it was wine.
But who ever saw one
or could tell a bat from the swifts
they sometimes flew with,
homing on insects those green evenings?
We never climbed the fence of Duffy's orchard
to catch them dog-toothed
sucking on his pears,
and the trouble was, as Duffy always said,
that in the dark you couldn't
recognize them for the leaves
and might reach up and get bit.
So the first time one of us found one
dead and held it open,
it looked like something crucified
to a busted umbrella,
the ribbed wings like a crackpot would make
to try and fly off of a dune.
As if it was made up of parts
of different animals, it had long bird-legs

stuck in lizard wrinkle pants,
and wire feet.
It wasn't even black, but brown and furry
with a puppy nose,
and when we threw it at each other
it wouldn't stick on anyone.
Then someone said his father knew somebody
who used to hunt between town and the back shore.
Coming home one night he ran across
a bat tree in the woods,
must have been hundreds folded upside down
pealing their single bell-notes through the dark.

Galvin takes us on a young person's learning journey, mixing lore about bats with emerging scientific facts. The bat is more than an ordinary mammal when we get up close and the poet has a good look for the first time. The outward description goes beyond basic observational data through his use of metaphor. The bat becomes more than bat:

it looked like something crucified
to a busted umbrella,
the ribbed wings like a crackpot would make
to try and fly off of a dune.
As if it was made up of parts
of different animals, it had long bird-legs
stuck in lizard wrinkle pants,
and wire feet.
It wasn't even black, but brown and furry. . . .

ACTION: FIND WAYS TO READ AND WRITE POETRY IN SCIENCE.

I find little difference between the way I look at the world through the eyes of a poet and the way I look at the world through the eyes of a scientist. I am confronted by many of the same questions: How come? Why did that happen? Should that have happened? What does that have to do with me? How can such elegance be described? What is the meaning of this? What's the evidence for that? What is the natural order in this event? I want to have a sense of scientific/poetic occasion as I consider the place of reading and writing poetry in the world of science.

Consider the wonder of the makeup of the universe I've just picked up three stones that I took from the top of Mount Washington in New Hampshire. I look at them carefully and I am struck at once by their variety. I know little of geology or of lichens and mosses. Oh, I can say, "That's moss, that's a lichen," but even if I couldn't identify them I would be struck by the fact that they are living organisms surviving on rocks at 6,300 feet and above the timberline. What I am trying to do here is look at these rocks with things growing on them as if for the first time. That is the way with poets and scientists— looking at the commonplace with fresh eyes. A rock is not just a rock.

Have the children go outside and pick up a rock that will be their rock. Ask them to study it and then try a list poem, as I will do now with my rock:

ROCK

Mica
glistens
bare
top
trees
green
side
gold
white
yellow
canyons
fuzz

> *lichens*
> *climb*
> *pitons*
> *hand*
> *over*
> *hand*
> *rope.*

In this list poem I let words trigger other words, but in column form. I take in the detail of my rock, barely one-and-one-quarter inches across and a half-inch high. I see the rock as if I am in a jet or helicopter looking down on it. The moss is treelike, and I see it as if it has its own timberline, since there is no moss on the top of the stone.

Suddenly I am a climber putting in pitons and working my way up my rock, hand over hand, with ropes around me. From a scientific point of view, through the medium of poetry, I recognize that moss can grow only on the side of this very small stone, the nonweather side. It may be a miniature mountain with its own "timberline." Poets, like scientists, constantly shift their point of view and examine their phenomena from all vantage points.

Examine the world in miniature   Use a microscope to encourage children to make the common uncommon. A crystal of salt, a bit of moss, a drop of water from a swamp, or a fly's leg open up a world of wonder in miniature. Children can try a list poem as a part of their initial observations.

Be sensitive to human issues in science   Complex problems such as deforestation, acid rain, the greenhouse effect, AIDS, and endangered species inspire complex emotions. Sometimes relevant poems can be an effective way to begin or end a unit or study area in science.

Look for repetition in the world   There is both science and beauty in repetition. I look at repetitions of structure in the gills of fish and lobster, and in the branching veins on the underside of a leaf, repetitions of color in birds and butterflies. I hear syncopation in the sound of a motor or a heartbeat under a stethoscope. Where there is motion there is often a repeating sound. Where there is structure, there is usually a repeating understructure to hold it together, such as the backbone, spinal column, ribs, and so on.

Ask big questions of little things

I look at a fly's leg under a microscope and see tiny hairs in abundance. I ask, "Why does a fly have all those tiny hairs? What is their purpose?" Immediately I begin to see how flies can easily carry bacteria from substances that become entangled in the hairs on their legs. "Why" questions, if pursued, lead us into larger questions.

Ask little questions of big things

In a way, little questions are more difficult to ask than big ones. Little questions provide the details that encourage an understanding of the larger question. I ask, "How can the issue of global warming be addressed?" Immediately I am confronted by a series of smaller questions: "What contributes to the warming?" "Do the people who contribute to it know about it?" "How can the chemistry and physics involved be described?"

Consider the world of motion

We live in a world of change. Poetry is a way of interpreting the world, whether in its human social-cultural dimension or its biological-physical dimension. Poets and scientists are careful to use precise words when they look at the world.

I am surrounded by motion and try a short poem, not quite a list, although it is like the list poem I did with the rock. I am going to concentrate on verbs.

MOTION
(FROM WHERE I SIT IN THE MOUNTAINS)
The wind puffs *from the north,*
my anemometer blinks *two miles an hour,*

while clouds ponder *their way south;*
Inside, my printer whirs *obedience,*
the amber light blinking *a faithful*
readiness, the inner electrons pulsating
messages, waiting *commands from my computer,*
the hard disk memory zigzagging *letters,*
words, slotting *them on a screen*
where a moving cursor trips *herky-jerky*
white letters on a blue background,
my fingers pulse *pianissimos*
to Rachmaninoff's Prelude in C-Sharp
minor, the fingers moving
from the command center
a cranial electronic storm,
a poem pushing *its way,*
my heart pumping, *the lungs*
eddying *air, while the sun*
heats *a snow-capped Washington*
and clouds form *their pink*
prelude to a new day.

That's a quick draft that embraces some of the motion going on around me. The verbs are highlighted to give a sense of the language of motion. Some of the verbs I like; some I don't. I don't care for "fingers moving." *Moving* is a weak verb, not very precise.

I write in response to my impressions. I move from weather to computers, CD players, my fingers composing, and back outside again to the new dawn that constantly changes shape on the mountaintops. To consider motion is to consider physics, but physics is more than physics as I begin to be aware of just a small part of this whirring universe. I discover emotion, beauty, and new elements I hadn't considered as being in motion.

ACTION: BRING POETRY INTO SOCIAL STUDIES.

If you bring poetry into the content areas, it is because you have a particular view about what it means to know and how literacy is connected with children's lives. The pace changes when you introduce poetry into social studies. You may not be able to cover all the content in the social studies curriculum. Poetry takes time. For example, you may focus on fewer years in American history, or one less continent in geography. Above all, you will seek to engage children in living history. Poetry has a place in this kind of curriculum.

Ken Burns, the producer of the popular series "The Civil War" on public television, recently (1990) gave the commencement address at the University of New Hampshire. He asked that we connect history with our own lives and become aware of our own participation in it. History is both past and present. To illustrate, he read from the eloquent letters of Civil War soldiers, many of whom were killed in battle. It is the present tense of their lives in these letters that links them to us today. Burns closed his address by reading a letter from Major Sullivan Ballou to his wife just before his death in the first battle of Bull Run. This impassioned letter shows how clearly poetry and history are interlaced. I will take the liberty of lining off part of the letter in the form of a poem without needing to change one word:

> *Sarah, my love for you is deathless,*
> *it seems to bind me with mighty cables*
> *that nothing but Omnipotence can break,*
> *and yet my love of country comes over me*
> *like a strong wind and bears me irresistibly*
> *with all those chains to the battlefield.*
>
> *The memory of all the blissful moments*
> *I have enjoyed with you come crowding*
> *over me, and I feel most deeply grateful*
> *to God and you that I have enjoyed*

them so long. And how hard it is for me
to give them up and burn to ashes
the hopes of future years when God
willing we might still have lived
and loved together and seen our boys
grown up to honorable manhood
around us . . . If I do not return,
my dear Sarah, never forget
how much I loved you, nor
that when my last breath escapes
me on the battlefield it will whisper
your name.

Forgive my many faults
and the many pains I have caused you,
how thoughtless, how foolish
I have sometimes been.
But Oh Sarah, if the dead can come
back to earth and flit unseen
around those they love,
I shall always be with you
in the brightest day
and the darkest night
always, always, and when the soft
breeze fans your cheek,
it shall be my breath,
or the cool air your throbbing
temple, it shall be my spirit
passing by. Sarah,
do not mourn me dead. Think
I am gone and wait for me
for we shall meet again.

When someone senses that they are a part of history and connected to other people in a special way, their use of language is affected. As Burns pointed out, history is not just the acts of presidents and generals. It is built on the backs of ordinary people. If we are to connect children to the world and to history itself, we must help them see themselves as participants.

ACTION: CONSIDER WAYS TO HELP CHILDREN PARTICIPATE IN HISTORY.

If children are to understand history they must understand that we see events from varied points of view. For example, the Civil War can be viewed through the eyes of privates, generals, mothers, wives, and children at home as well as through those of statesmen and people of other nations. There are opposing points of view not only among the antagonists but among those on the same side. For the following Action opportunities, you will need to supply examples for the details in your curriculum where they can be applied:

- Imagine yourself as a character in history (e.g., Robert E. Lee) and write a poem. Try one stanza from one side, the next stanza from an opposing point of view (e.g., Ulysses S. Grant). Of course, another option would be to write a poem where both held the same point of view.
- Examine an issue and write a poem in class where children provide specific examples for each of the following more abstract issues:
  - Poverty.
  - War.
  - Peace.
  - Great decisions.
  - Blunders.
  - Heroes.
  - Your own family history.
  - Discovery.
  - Invention.
  - Argument.
  - Injustice.
  - Social conflict.

• Bring the daily newspaper to class and have children select an article to write a poem about. Encourage them to consider their own personal reaction or knowledge of the event as they write. Try writing this poem with the children.

ACTION: CONSIDER THE PLACE OF MATHEMATICS AND POETRY.

Mathematics, like poetry, expresses complex ideas in symbolic ways. They both attempt to order and understand reality and experience. During my reading of *Living and Learning Mathematics* by David Whitin and his colleagues, I was struck by a section of prose (p. 6) in which I found an embedded poem:

> *Mathematics is for*
> *recipes to be doubled,*
> *plants to be measured,*
> *fruit to be divided,*
> *prices to be compared,*
> *polls to be interpreted,*
> *time to be estimated,*
> *meals to be ordered,*
> *bills to be paid,*
> *and marbles to be shared.*

Within each of these lines there is a potential story, and within each story a person and an event. Numbers are always more than numbers.

ACTION: MAKE A LIST OF ALL THE DIFFERENT TIMES YOU USED NUMBERS YESTERDAY.

I look forward to trying this one with you. Subconsciously, I know I am a number person in spite of my more frequent involvement in descriptive research. I'll jot down a list and then try to write a poem from it:

- Checked clock for time.
- Checked temperature inside and outside.
- Checked wind velocity and direction on my anemometer.
- Turned on computer and punched in number for my Word-Perfect on hard disk.
- Inserted date for new disk file, punched in numbers for margins, spacing.
- Punched in numbers for at least six to eight phone calls.
- Checked totals in columns for income tax.
- Wrote check from checkbook. Subtracted.
- Punched in numbers on microwave for heating coffee, for baking potato.
- Estimated number of plays for Oakland for ball control in last two minutes of playoff game with Cincinnati.
- Shared correct time with person while skiing.
- Estimated distance to determine the time I wanted to be out cross-country skiing.
- Measured coffee and water for making coffee.
- Set time before turning food over in fry pan.
- Punched in number on CD player for late night listening to Bach's Toccata and Fugue in D Minor. Checked length of selection. Adjusted volume to right level.
- Estimated amount of wood needed to fill wood rack next to stove.
- Looked at heat gauge on car dashboard to check if I should put on the heater.
- Looked over statistics for both the Bears-Giants game and the Oakland-Cincinnati game.
- Checked my weight at the end of the day.
- Estimated amount of toothpaste needed for toothbrush.

I'd better stop there for fear of becoming boring. On the other hand, I am fascinated by how many estimates and calculations we make in the course of a day. I suspect I am unaware of countless other quantitative judgments I have not recorded here. Along with each quantitative judgment is a qualitative one: ''Is this significant?''

I look over my list to see if a poem is embedded in the quantitative judgments I have made during the day. I see a few possibilities as I look for patterns, issues, and stories:

- My orientation to the day is numerical, mostly connected to temperature.
- I use numbers a lot with my computer.
- The day involves frequent estimates: cross-country skiing, CD disk, heat gauge, football plays.

I think I'll explore how I use numbers to begin the day. Here is a quick first draft.

WHERE AM I?

Tap the barometer,
the arrow drops,
low pressure on the move,
check the temperature,
fourteen degrees,
the dawn just peeking
clear and cold,
a trace of cirrus
at 45,000 feet,
an oncoming storm,
weather on the march,
and I feel tectonic plates
shift uneasily beneath
the geosynclines,
they've been rumbling
and bubbling for aeons,
before the Revolution,
the pyramids, the stone
age, before the first grunt
of Ogg. And I, I am a mite,

an afterthought, a microsecond,
who checks his watch
to see if the roast
is done, the game won,
the 24-second clock beaten,
the car warm enough,
the thermostat working,
somehow I have to know the score
if the day is worth starting.

I like this first draft. I'll return to it to polish and rework some of my discoveries. I'm still a little puzzled about all my checking routines. There's something underneath it all that's worth exploring. I have a hunch as I read this draft (which guarantees that I will pursue successive drafts) that I have an urge to influence time; if I know how time manifests itself, I can either control it or be in greater harmony with it.

Mathematics explores space and time. Einstein puzzled over their relationship. In fact, his understanding of relativity came from a *metaphorical insight* before he calculated it mathematically.

For this Action, then, make a list of your own use of numbers in a twenty-four-hour period. What do you learn about yourself as you reexamine your list? Do you see patterns? Take a pattern or a particular use of numbers and write a five- to ten-minute poem. Then look at your first draft to see how you might approach a second draft.

ACTION: EXAMINE OTHER WAYS TO USE POETRY AND MATHEMATICS.

Throughout this examination of poetry and content subjects my intent has been to reconnect children with their world. For younger children, work together as a class as you recall together the ways in which quantitative judgments were made during your day together. Older students should be able to keep diaries of their own. Show what you mean by a quantitative diary with a few entries from your own to help them begin their diary. Some other ways to link poetry and math are the following:

- Connect yourself to a favorite number and compose a poem of recall.
- Write a poem in which a number worked for you.
- Write a poem in which a number worked against you.
- Write a poem that is predictive of amount.
- Consider some of these first lines for poems:
  - I remember the time the bag broke . . .
  - Three days to Valentine's day . . .
  - Four people and only two tickets to the game . . .
  - I think I put too much soap in the washer . . .
  - My dog had twelve puppies . . .
  - We are behind by four runs in the seventh inning and there are only two innings left . . .

ACTION: CONSIDER THE VISUAL ARTS AS AREAS FOR WRITING POETRY.

Poetry has much in common with the visual arts. Both are art forms in which the artist tries to say more than is immediately evident to the senses. It is quite common to find writers who are heavily involved in other arts. You may find it useful to read *Doubly Gifted: The Writer as Visual Artist* (Hjerter 1986). I am not focusing on the "gifted." Rather, my point is that it is quite natural to express oneself in more than one art form.

If I seek to express more than the mere surface of things in order to explore new meanings, I do not need to confine myself to words. I can naturally move into music, oils, acrylics, clay, photography, woodworking, weaving, sewing, and so on. The processes in each are similar. I compose in order to find out what I think and to express something beyond this moment.

Linda Rief (1991), an eighth-grade teacher at Oyster River Middle School in Durham, New Hampshire, had children focus on issues that were important to them: the Holocaust, drugs, and homelessness. They read novels and eyewitness accounts, kept notes, and then prepared to express themselves in various media. What was clear to Rief and her students was that each art form enhanced the other. The students continued to interweave their discoveries, finding one understanding in art, another in writing.

Mekeel McBride, a nationally known poet, asked students in her poetry class to provide some form of musical accompaniment with the reading of their poems. The interpretation of what "accompaniment" meant ranged from a poem about an automobile, which the student read standing next to the car with the engine running, to a poem about a painful personal experience in which the student rubbed the edge of a wine glass with a moist cloth, producing an excruciating, high-pitched sound.

Consider some of the following approaches to using poetry in the arts:

- Listen for music in the sound of machines and other moving things. Compose a poem that includes sound effects.
- Choose a subject that interests you and about which you have passionate feelings. Read about it with an eye to representing a central idea using paint, clay, fabric, or other materials. Experiment with a quick five-minute poem before, during, or after your construction.
- Choose an art object. Write a poem expressing the essence of the object, representing it with the clear pictures it triggers in your mind.

ACTION: CONSIDER THE WORLD OF SPORT AND THE WRITING OF POETRY.

I am an unapologetic, unabashed sports nut. I was raised in the household of a coach-educator. My father took my brother and me to Yankee stadium, Ebbets field, Polo Grounds, and Fenway Park before we were ten; we traveled to state basketball tournaments, read the sports page each morning, threw basketballs, baseballs, and footballs in season, and debated ad nauseum the significance of certain statistical achievements.

Sports belong to poetry. The verb of exquisite motion and human drama requires poets who can do justice to the becoming of the players in all the sports. A score is more than a score. A drama has unfolded whether it be a home run with the bases loaded or a three-way race across the playground by four second graders. The drama ends; the poet observes, goes to her seat, takes out a piece of paper, and lives the moment again for herself and all the other children.

Verbs blaze in the neon world of sports. Motion is sports; sports is motion. Motion with grace, motion with ragged determination and grotesque purpose, motion with drama: sports is the verb personified. It is a poetic domain. Here is Stephen Dunn's poem "Outfielder":

> *So this is excellence; movement*
> *toward the barely possible—*
> *the puma's dream*
> *of running down a hummingbird*
> *on a grassy plain.*

Or Carl Lindner's basketball poem, "When I Got it Right":

> *The ball would lift*
> *light as a wish,*
> *gliding like a blessing*
> *over the rim, pure,*
> *or kissing off glass*
> *into the skirt of net.*
> *Once it began*
> *I couldn't miss.*
> *Even in the falling dark,*
> *the ball, before it left*
> *my hand, was sure.*

Things are never quite what they seem. In this instance, in the hands of the poet, a fly ball is not just a fly ball, nor a shot just a swisher. The person is inextricably connected in grace and passion with the ball in flight. Sports belong to the poet. Catch the universality of baseball in Emilio De Grazia's "Pastime":

> *A girl, nine years of wonder*
> *Still on her face,*
> *Stands directly on the bag at third*
> *Running amazed fingers along the wrinkles*
> *Of my old leather mitt.*
> *It is the bottom of the ninth,*
> *And everywhere in the world*
> *The bases are loaded.*

Children are deeply involved in the drama of sports. At recess they swing on the bars, play kickball, baseball, or football, or jump rope. With the active verbs of sport go the metaphors. Sport involves so much becoming and acting in the middle of dramatic moments that metaphors spring from the writing like fish jumping for flies.

Observe children at play during recess, pick up on the activity, and show what you saw in a poem as an example when they come inside. I wrote this poem for children who were playing kickball.

> *KICKBALL*
>
> *Michael planted one foot*
> *like he wouldn't budge*
> *it in a hurricane, stuck*
> *out his tongue, and swung*
> *that other leg like he'd rip*
> *rubber right off the ball,*
> *and BOOM a sound was heard*
> *clear into Ms. Winter's*
> *room; the ball sailed*

high like something shot
from a cannon down at the circus;
Michael pumped around those bases,
laughing and waving his arms
like recess would go on for hours
and hours, and he didn't care
if he ever got to home plate,
just so home runs would never end.

Every morning there are little dramas on the playground before school, at recess, or at lunch: small races, chases, ball throwing, catching, imagining, taunts, victories, and defeats. These are all actions that belong to poetry.

FINAL REFLECTION   Poetry is not a genre "on a hill," nor should it be confined to writing time, English, or Language Arts. Poetry is for thinking and feeling. It is the deep yearning to express thoughts and emotions that moves people of all ages to write poetry.

This book has been a side-by-side journey in which I have written poetry with you and you have written poetry with your children, and the children have written with and for each other. Poetry is a studio subject in which the teacher works and explores the craft alongside the students. We read poetry and experience the common, which becomes uncommon in the hands of the poet. We write poetry and discover surprises around the bend of every line.

appendix   I have included the following poems for those readers interested in the kinds of poems I have written over the last four
years.

SUNDAY AT THE LAKE

This quiet lake feeds
a shore of hemlock, cedar
and fir; no sound, save
cicadas and crickets,
a child at play, but now

male marauders open
throttle, their spark plugs
snapping a deep-throat
delight and like canines
pissing their territory
spray contempt with great
gouts of bow waves gone
mad, waves that slap
at kayak, canoe and sail
with only arms and wind
to move them through
the waiting water,
and in the evening

when they put their engines
to bed, they power
beneath the sheets,
hoping their ramming
pulsing surges will ignite
the last loud cry
of the day, their bow waves
to smack the walls,
the screens, this lake
that silently sobs
a cool, cleansing wash.

CANDLES

"I wanna blow,
I wanna blow."
five year old cheeks
poised and full
purse wide-eyed
for the plunge
of extinguishing
the after-dinner flames
of two candles set
in brass, their wax
dripping down the sides
of an evening well spent
in dinner, doddling
and stories and
as I said
his cheeks were full,
and whooshed their
optimism in great
gusts of diffusion
the candle unwilling
to allow even childish
folly, fairly flickers.

Great grandmother, her
own flame low
in the evening,
the oxygen missing
the elevator to memory
stuck somewhere
between pulmonary
and carotid, in a sweet,
shy smile places
a hand behind
that prissy flame,

to transform those errant puffs
into childish joy,
the shouts of power
giggling his sides
while time stops still
in a naked, blackened,
stub of a wick
that great grandmother
unknowing, sees.

SOUTHEAST WIND

The southeast wind
puffs grey rain
and I hear mourning
from the dove
that pecks the last
cracked corn
before the flag
starts to beat
its dirge against
the hollow, metal
pole; now clouds,
like lumbering elephants,
ponder their way,
then inch, one foot
after another, hauling
the horizon and all
its entourage
of heart-weeping reunions,
grounded sailboats,
and a flag-draped caisson
toward the sallow, yellow
glow in the West.

RAIN DANCE

Giggling savages,
their bodies naked,
and shimmering like foals
prancing under rainbows
in the afternoon
rain, they leap,

bodies splayed
into the to and fro
arc of a lawn sprinkler,
then stop, pivot,
and thrust their bottoms,
to tee-hee the tickle
of cascading beads
of water, then

dash again, skipping
in the short, wet grass
to face their spraying
oppressor with eyes
wide over jack-o-lantern
mouths, thrust chins, and
lallygagging tongues, then

tip-toe with little
prissy steps to leap
like circus ponies through
the hoops of rain,
their curtain of coolness
on a hot July afternoon
in New Hampshire.

THE RED CARPET CLUB

There are no birds
in these Friendly Skies
just computers spitting
their graphics
in five color array;
a cigar-smoking mover
in grey suit
scorns his seat,
stretches his cord
and stomps huffy consonants
down the SPRINT fibre
optics runway to close
a deal in Detroit.

No gold finches
here strutting their
April spring clothes,
just the chink, chink
of cups on saucers;
the Wall Street Journal
says gold is a bad
investment this year,
the market too slippery
for the private investor;
sell your soul
to the future,
big houses, good return
CDs in Texas,
good return. The future
is now; you deserve
palm trees, low taxes,
fresh pineapple
and slithery women
who deliver martinis

at the pool bar;
so invest, close, fly
the Friendly Skies;

I'm a card-carrying
Mileage Plus, Premier,
first-boarding, no-shit
at-the-door, deserving
grabber, whose future
is in privilege,
membership, free coffee,
a smile, and my name
announced at the door
of the Red Carpet Club
where finches can't bother
me, their songs don't
sell, and their flights
never do leave on time anyway.

GREAT WHITE HERON

White spike in a mangrove,
luminescent, crystaline,
a platform balanced between
heaven and heart.

Living spear,
it strides
one suspended step
after another:
cool ivory,
cold logic,
stately step,
stalking stiletto.

The head cocks,
a white bowstring, slowly
drawn, tight with the tension
of the moment when a minnow swims
into the crosshairs of the knowing eye.
The head fires;
Fish.

ON YOUR SILENCES
(FOR DAN LING FU)

Silent, so silent,
just the murmur
of your breathing,
a quiet breeze
in pines,
as if in the stillness
you can hear
your own thoughts,
the swan that sails
across your mind,
the swan who wonders
why people scurry
like restless rabbits
on the shore.

FOG

Fog hangs in treetops
tasting spruce gum
and inhaling the tang
of low tide.

Bored, it calls
for west wind
and leaves like witches brew
in morning sunshine.

CONVERSATION

We stood in the doorway
opening up memories
like you'd open up
the little drawers
that go from floor
to ceiling down at Sampson's
General Store.

THE VERB OF FOG

The verb of fog is a grey elephant
with marshmallow thoughts
mumbling apologies for a nothing day.

The verb of fog fears fatigue,
facing an empty, king-sized bed
smooth with the possibility of love . . .

The verb of fog steams before guerilla
shadows darting around campfires
somewhere between Minsk and Smolensk.

The verb of fog hangs like Irish lace
over father's eyes; he says, "I can't
seem to decide where the bathroom is."

MORNING SNOW

*Now in the quiet
reach of aspens
and firs, the first
filmy whispers
of patient flakes
flower their blessing
on the rude
remnants of yesterday.*

references

Blishen, Edward, ed. 1984. *Oxford Book of Poetry for Children*. Illustrations by Brian Wildsmith. New York: Peter Bedrick Books.

Burns, Kenneth. 1990. Commencement address. Durham: University of New Hampshire.

Denman, Gregory A. 1988. *When You've Made It Your Own . . .* Portsmouth, N. H.: Heinemann.

Drake, Barbara. 1983. *Writing Poetry*. New York: Harcourt Brace Jovanovich.

Graves, Donald H. 1990. *Discover Your Own Literacy*. Portsmouth, N.H.: Heinemann.

Greenfield, Eloise. 1978. *Honey I Love*. Illustrated by Diane and Leo Dillon. New York: HarperCollins Publishers.

Grennan, Eamon. 1989. *What Light There Is*. San Francisco, Calif.: North Point Press.

Heard, Georgia. 1989. *For the Good of the Earth and Sun*. Portsmouth, N. H.: Heinemann.

Heller, Ruth. 1982. *Animals Born Alive and Well*. New York: Grosset and Dunlap, Inc.

———. 1984. *Plants that Never Ever Bloom*. New York: Grosset and Dunlap, Inc.

———. 1986. *The Reason for a Flower*. New York: Grosset and Dunlap, Inc.

IIjerter, Kathleen. 1986. *Doubly Gifted: The Writer as Visual Artist*. New York: Harry N. Abrams, Inc.

Hopkins, Lee Bennett. 1987. *Pass the Poetry Please*. New York: HarperCollins Publishers.

———. 1988. *Side by Side: Poems to Read Together*. Illustrated by Hillary Knight. New York: HarperCollins Publishers.

Kennedy, X. J., and Dorothy Kennedy. 1982. *Knock at a Star*. Boston: Little, Brown and Co.

Lattimore, Richard. 1972. *Poems from Three Decades*. Chicago: University of Chicago Press.

McBride, Mckeel. *Red Letter Days*. Pittsburgh, Pa.: Carnegie Mellon University Press. 1988.

McLuhan, Marshall. 1966. *Understanding Media*. New York: Signet.

Newkirk, Thomas, and Nancie Atwell, eds. 1988. *Understanding Writing: Ways of Observing, Learning, and Teaching K–8*. 2nd ed. Portsmouth, N. H.: Heinemann.

Rief, Linda. 1992. *Seeking Diversity: Language Arts with Adolescents*. Portsmouth, N. H.: Heinemann.

Schenk, Beatrice, ed. 1988. *Sing a Song of Popcorn*. New York: Scholastic Books, Inc.

Thomas, Lewis. 1983. *Late Night Thoughts on Listening to Mahler's Ninth Symphony*. New York: Penguin USA.

Wallace, Robert. 1982. *Writing Poems*. Boston: Little, Brown and Co.

Index